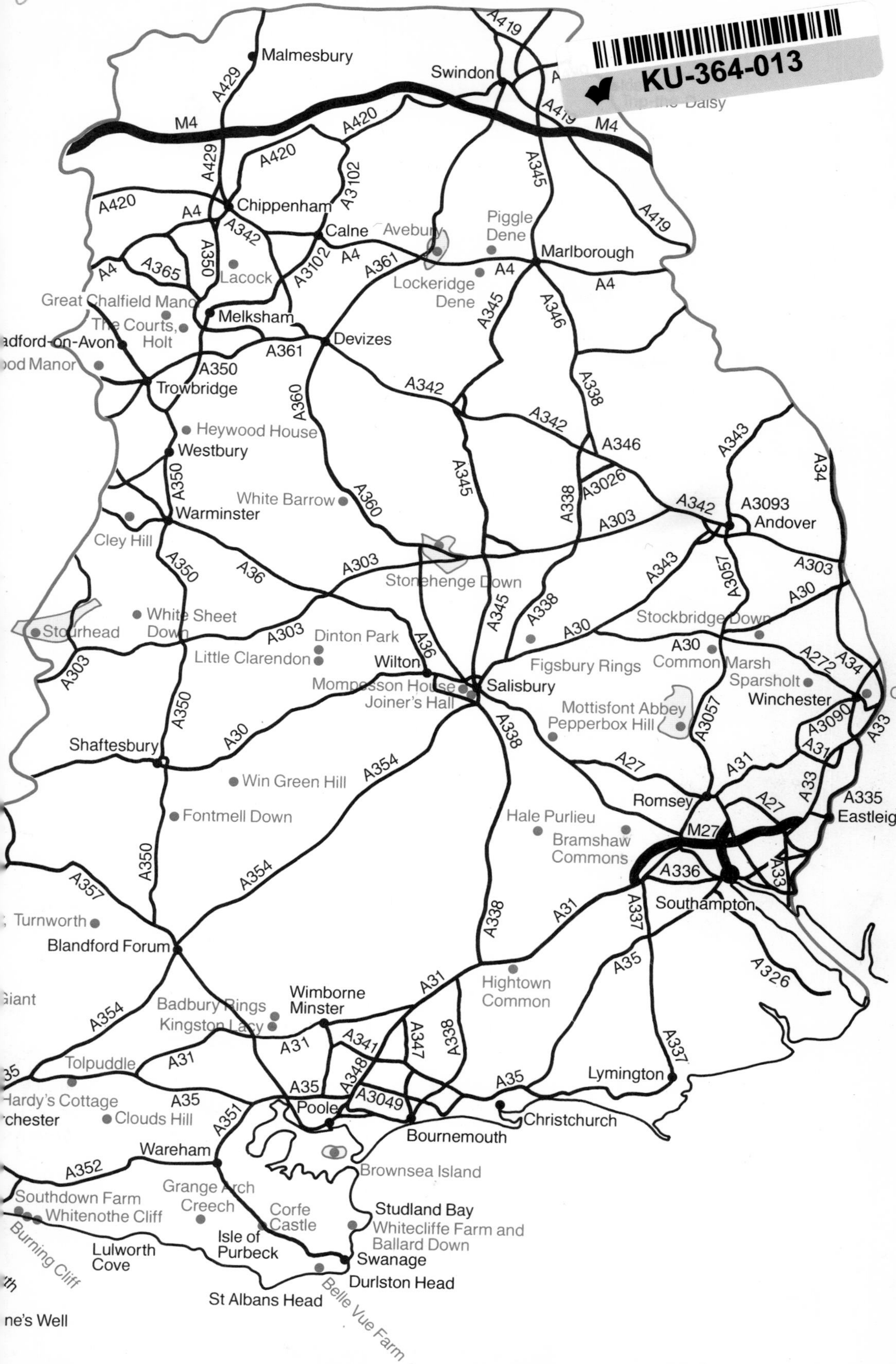
Malmesbury
Swindon
A419
M4
A429
A420
A3102
Chippenham
A4
A342
Calne
Avebury
Piggle Dene
Marlborough
A350
Lacock
A365
A361
Lockeridge Dene
A345
A346
Great Chalfield Manor
The Courts, Holt
Melksham
Devizes
adford-on-Avon
ood Manor
Trowbridge
A360
A338
A343
Heywood House
Westbury
A3026
A34
White Barrow
Warminster
A303
A3093
Andover
Cley Hill
A36
A3057
Stonehenge Down
White Sheet Down
Stourhead
Dinton Park
Little Clarendon
A30
Stockbridge Down
Common Marsh
Wilton
Figsbury Rings
A272
Mompesson House
Joiner's Hall
Salisbury
Sparsholt
Winchester
City Mill
Mottisfont Abbey
Pepperbox Hill
A3090
A33
Shaftesbury
A27
A31
A354
Win Green Hill
Romsey
A335
Eastleigh
Fontmell Down
Hale Purlieu
Bramshaw Commons
M27
A336
Southampton
A337
A357
Turnworth
Blandford Forum
A326
A35
Hightown Common
Giant
Badbury Rings
Kingston Lacy
Wimborne Minster
A341
A347
Tolpuddle
A348
Lymington
Hardy's Cottage
Clouds Hill
Poole
A3049
Christchurch
chester
A351
Bournemouth
Wareham
A352
Brownsea Island
Southdown Farm
Whitenothe Cliff
Grange Arch
Creech
Corfe Castle
Studland Bay
Whitecliffe Farm and Ballard Down
Burning Cliff
Lulworth Cove
Isle of Purbeck
Swanage
Durlston Head
St Albans Head
Belle Vue Farm
ne's Well

'In these Wessex nooks the busy outsider's ancient times are only old; his old times are still new; his present is futurity.'
Thomas Hardy, *Far From the Madding Crowd*

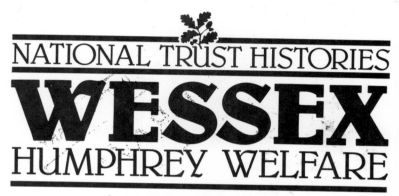

NATIONAL TRUST HISTORIES
WESSEX
HUMPHREY WELFARE

Series Editor Richard Muir

Willow Books
Collins
Grafton Street, London
in association with
The National Trust
1984

For Nicky,
Becky, William and Pippa

Willow Books
William Collins & Co Ltd
London Glasgow Sydney Auckland
Toronto Johannesburg

Welfare, Humphrey
Wessex.
(National Trust
regional history series)
1. Wessex (England) – Description
and travel
I. Title II. Series
914.23 DA670.W48

Hardback ISBN 0 00 218111 8
Paperback ISBN 0 00 218112 6

First published 1984
Copyright © 1984 Humphrey Welfare

Made by Lennard Books
Mackerye End, Harpenden,
Herts AL5 5DR

Editor Michael Leitch
Designed by David Pocknell's Company Ltd
Production Reynolds Clark Associates Ltd
Printed and bound in Spain by
TONSA, San Sebastian

Cover Photographs

Centre: Avebury

Top left: West Kennet Long Barrow

Top right: Stonehenge

CONTENTS

EDITOR'S INTRODUCTION

Wessex takes its name from the West Saxon kingdom which, in the reign of Alfred the Great and his successors, provided the core from which English statehood and nationalism could expand. This was not the first time that Wessex had assumed a central position on the British stage, for in the Neolithic and early Bronze Age periods it emerged as a rich and innovative region with a sophisticated and dynamic organization which is still proclaimed by world-famous monuments such as Stonehenge, Avebury and Silbury Hill.

At the mention of the word 'Wessex', the thoughts of most readers will turn to Stonehenge and to the regional novels of Thomas Hardy. Sadly, the ploughing-up of the traditional downland pastures and the removal of ancient hedgerows, woodlands and wetlands from the vales have radically changed some of Hardy's windswept grasslands and dairy-rich lowlands. Even so, Wessex still contains some fine countryside and a wealth of monuments of different ages. Beside the glories of the prehistoric legacy, the area contains such great churches as Salisbury Cathedral and Sherborne Abbey, famous mansions such as Wilton and Longleat, remarkable fortresses such as Portland and Corfe Castles, fascinating villages such as Lacock and Milton Abbas as well as important industrial monuments such as those in Bradford-on-Avon and Swindon.

In this book Humphrey Welfare explains the creation of the Wessex landscape and introduces a wonderful assemblage of monuments and settlements to demonstrate that the region contains an inexhaustible legacy of interesting places, some of them well-known and much-visited, but many more which are usually overlooked by the visitor. The author is a graduate of Newcastle University and is employed as an Investigator with the Royal Commission on Historical Monuments. He has a special understanding of the antiquities of the Wessex landscape as for several years, preceding his very recent transfer to the North–East, he was based in Salisbury and engaged in surveying and recording the monuments of the area. He is the author of several specialist publications on late prehistoric and Roman Britain and is the co-author of the *National Trust Guide to Prehistoric and Roman Britain.*

Richard Muir
Great Shelford, 1983

THE LANDSCAPE AND EARLY MAN

Wessex exists chiefly in the mind, defying exact definition of its boundaries. For many people it is the chalk downland, for others the landscape of Thomas Hardy and W. H. Hudson, a rich Bronze Age culture, or an Anglo-Saxon kingdom. It is all these things, but in this book Wessex is regarded as Dorset, Wiltshire (excluding the Cotswold edge and the Thames Valley north of Swindon), and Hampshire west of Winchester. The New Forest is included but the Isle of Wight, although geologically a part of Wessex, has a wholly separate identity.

Two centuries ago the majority of the British population lived in the countryside, enjoying an intimate relationship with the land. In many regions of England these close ties have been swept away, but one of the great charms of Wessex is that it is still predominantly a rural area, where the inhabitant or returning native can feel near to his roots.

The region contains some of the greatest variety of countryside in southern England: whaleback chalk downland, warm and fertile clay vales, the heaths and woodlands of south-east Dorset and the New Forest, the high cliffs bounding Lyme Bay, and the sands and mudflats around Poole Harbour.

This variety pleases the eye but it is more deeply founded than that. It is all too easy for those not directly connected with the land to forget how much the underlying geology affects the way we live. It dictates the form of the landscape; the natural flora and fauna; the fertility of the soil; the distribution of arable farms, of pasture, woodland and heaths; the availability of water supplies and the position of settlements; the success of extractive and many manufacturing industries; the building materials used locally and thus, until very recently, even the colours of our villages and towns.

For many people, however, the Wessex landscape is synonymous in the mind's eye with chalk downs and combes: smoothly rounded contours, flint-studded arable fields and closely-cropped sheep pastures, with some of the higher hills crowned with a prehistoric hill fort or a clump of trees. Chalk does indeed predominate, for it forms the foundation of Salisbury Plain, of central Hampshire and the Marlborough Downs, with an outstretched arm extending southwards into Dorset.

The chalk downs as they used to be: Heddington to the north of Devizes in the early eighteenth century. The high pastures contrast with the small enclosed fields and woods of the clay lowlands.

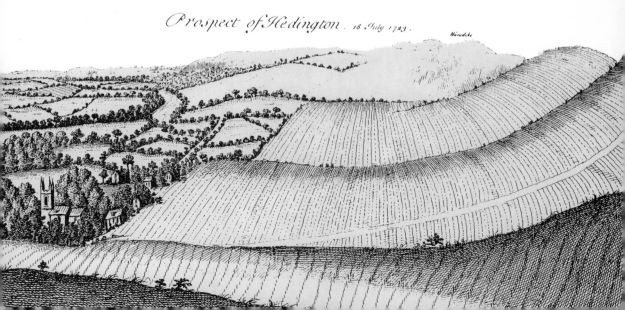

Prospect of Hedington. 18 July 1723.

The geology of Wessex may be imagined as a white apron – the chalk – held out to gather the newer and softer rocks of the Hampshire basin. The outer hem of the apron reappears on its southern side as the thin strip of downland that runs eastwards through the Isle of Purbeck and the Isle of Wight. In the great earth-movements that produced the Alps, the chalk that was to form central southern England was folded downwards, enabling much of the Solent hinterland to fill up with younger rocks, mostly sands and clays. The chalk was tilted southwards and eroded in such a way that its abrupt northern edge is marked by a chain of high and windswept escarpments. These dominate the clay lowlands to the north, with views that can be best appreciated from Barbury Castle on the Marlborough Downs, from the White Horse above Westbury, and all along the southern edge of Blackmoor Vale. The hedgerowed landscape of rich clay meadows and ploughlands contrasts sharply with the wide sweeps of the chalk, with its steep pastures below the crest of the escarpment and huge modern arable fields on the gentler slopes behind.

The chalk itself is a soft white marine limestone composed largely of calcium carbonate from the remains of planktonic algae and the shells of other tiny creatures who lived and died in the seas about 100 million years ago. The skeletons of sponges in this Chalk Sea were the source of silica, an insoluble substance which has been left behind in the chalk. We find it today as flint, the black glassy rock that was so essential to prehistoric man as a raw material for his tools; in a landscape short of stone, flint later became invaluable as a building material.

Though the chalk is quick to drain, it can hold water like a sponge wherever it lies over impermeable rocks. The deep valleys or 'combes' between the downs may have been carved during the

glaciations ('Ice Ages') that affected the rest of Britain. Many combes are now 'dry valleys' that contain streams only during the wetter months of the winter. The common place-name Winterbourne is a sign of these fickle watercourses.

Nevertheless, although they cannot be said to be grand, some of the rivers of Wessex are fine indeed. Their charm as landscape lies in the intimacy of meadows merging into bulrushes and water crowfoot, the dark silhouettes of salmon and trout motionless against the sharp flints of the riverbeds. It will surprise many to learn that this riverine landscape is almost wholly man-made and that the true course of the rivers is often difficult to guess from the ground. The Itchen, the Test and the Salisbury Avon meander along the gravel floors of their valleys, their courses frayed into separate strands by man. Like the Stour and the Frome in Dorset they have been diverted and channelled in the past to provide water-meadows and to power flour mills; now one of their chief economic values lies in their clear chalk water, highly prized by fish and fishermen alike.

Where the chalk has been worn away to expose the underlying Gault clays and Greensands, the contrasts with the downland are marked. An example is the Vale of Pewsey, running west to Devizes, which has an almost level floor used by the Kennet and Avon Canal, and bounded by high chalk escarpments to both north and south. The Vale of Wardour, between Salisbury and Shaftesbury, was formed in the same way but is a more broken, wooded countryside. It is not only in the lowlands that this contrast can appear, for pockets of 'clay-with-flints' (red or chocolate-coloured clay containing flint pebbles), left as remnants on the highest chalk hills, often produce woodlands like those along the Grovely ridge.

To the south of a line running roughly through Romsey,

Above: The view towards Westbury along the steep northern edge of the chalk escarpment. Greensand outcrops along the foot of the slopes merge into the flat claylands beyond.
Left: The deeply indented wooded combes on the western edge of Cranborne Chase near Fontmell Magna, where the chalk downs fall steeply to the lower slopes of Greensand and clays.
The strip-lynchets seen on the left were still part of the village's medieval open-field system in 1774.

The gentle flow of the Test at Horsebridge near King's Somborne; for fishermen this river is one of the most prized stretches of water in southern England.

Fordingbridge, Wimborne, Dorchester and Swanage, the dipping chalk is covered by the younger sands and clays. Where left in their natural state these are covered by the heathlands and woodlands of the New Forest, of east Dorset and Purbeck. From the crest of Ballard Down in the Isle of Purbeck many of these contrasts are immediately visible. The smooth, pastured outline of the Down itself is part of the narrow chalk ridge, breached at Corfe Castle, that meets the sea at Old Harry Rocks, to reappear again on the Isle of Wight as The Needles. To the north, behind the dunes of Studland Bay, stretch the low-lying sandy heaths around Poole Harbour, now clothed with conifer plantations. To the south of Ballard Down, softer clays have been eroded to produce the valley that emerges in Swanage Bay, while further south again the hard Purbeck and Portland limestones appear as a high plateau ending in Peveril Point and Durlston Head.

Westwards along the coast, the rather barren Isle of Portland has been terribly scarred by quarrying. The views, however, can be magnificent, taking in the 16 miles (26 km) of Chesil Beach all the way to Bridport. The pebbles on this extraordinary offshore beach are graded by Nature, being the size of oranges near Portland, but only of peas at the western end. Between Burton Bradstock and Lyme Regis the clays, limestones, shales and sandstones of the ancient Lias rocks, famous for their fossils, are exposed in the cliffs. Where capped by Greensand, as at Black Ven, Stonebarrow, Golden Cap and Thorncombe Beacon, these cliffs tower about 630 ft (190 m) above Lyme Bay.

Inland lies Marshwood

The shading emphasizes the higher ground, mainly chalk downland, that contrasts with the clay vales to the north, and with the relatively low-lying heathlands of the New Forest and eastern Dorset.

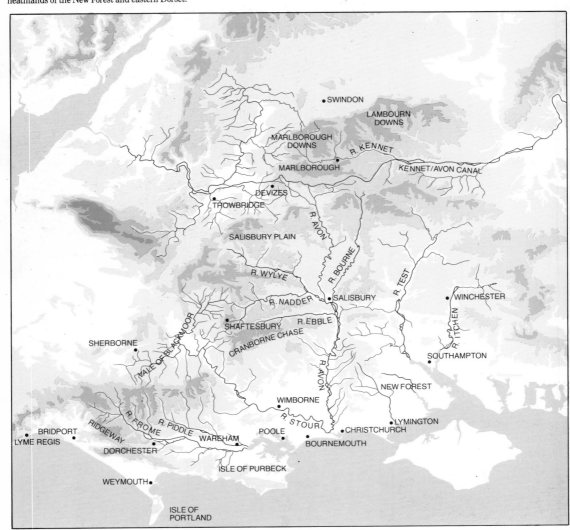

Vale with its wooded and well-watered heavy clay soils: a secret landscape hidden from most of the casual summer visitors heading for Charmouth and Lyme Regis. A more accessible clay lowland, in the north-west of Dorset between Sherborne and Shaftesbury, is the Vale of Blackmoor – dairy country, where villages like Marnhull and Hinton St Mary huddle on small knolls, as if to keep their feet out of the water. Viewed from the chalk escarpment to the south – from above Buckland Newton, from Bulbarrow, or Hambledon Hill – the Vale seems to merge almost imperceptibly into the haze of distant Somerset.

Above right: The high cliffs of the Golden Cap estate, looking eastwards around the broad sweep of Lyme Bay to Chesil Beach and the Isle of Portland (upper right). The good sheep pastures were to be of enormous importance to Wessex.

Right: Lulworth Cove, where the sea has breached the strip of limestone extending along the coast, to cut into the softer clays behind. The crest of the long chalk ridge (top left) carries the rampart of the huge and unusual Iron Age hill fort of Bindon, which enclosed the cove and the coastal shelf beyond.

Below: Lyme Regis in 1723, with Golden Cap, Thorncombe Beacon and the Isle of Portland beyond. Landslips are constantly reshaping this coastline: St Michael's Church now stands on the edge of the sea, and the medieval harbour wall ('the Cobb') has been frequently destroyed and rebuilt.

The First Settlers

For the greater part of his history in Britain the presence of man is only known through the flint tools he left behind him. Faced with rows of these simple objects lying in museum cases it is sometimes easy to forget that they were made by tough but sensitive men and women, struggling as a tiny minority among the other animals in an environment that was often hostile. It was to be a long battle.

The ancestors of modern man may have arrived in Wessex between about 700,000 and 350,000 years ago. Behind their prominent brows these short muscular individuals carried the knowledge to use fire and fashion crude pebble tools. The flint gravels of the Hampshire basin were especially attractive for this. On their sporadic and seasonal visits over the land-bridge from the continent their small hunting parties tracked down deer, ox, elephant, rhinoceros and wild horses. Some more permanent settlement probably took place during the warmer climatic phases, but this would be difficult to prove.

Much of the evidence for these earliest periods has been swept away, not only by modern farming and developments but also in antiquity, during the glaciations that ebbed and flowed over Northern Europe. Usually the early flint tools are found singly but small concentrations, dating from a warm period between 300 000 and 200 000 BC, have turned up on Milford Hill and at Bemerton on the outskirts of Salisbury, and at Little Bedwyn near Marlborough. Much later, about 90 000 – 75 000 BC, Neanderthal man visited central southern England, leaving his simple tools behind him at Fisherton in Salisbury, at Christchurch, and at Warsash and Lepe on the shores of Southampton Water.

The enormous time-scales of early prehistory are underlined by the relatively recent appearance in Wessex of 'modern' man, between about 45,000 and 35,000 years ago. He heralded the period known to archaeologists as the Upper Paleolithic (Old Stone Age), bringing with him characteristic leaf-shaped spear-points of a type that have been found at Christchurch. More than 20,000 years, and a severe glaciation, had to pass before the final Paleolithic phase: this lasted from about 12,000 to 10,000 years ago. The cold and inhospitable glacial tundra with its mosses, lichens, grasses, and dwarf strains of birch and willow, gradually gave way to pine and hazel as the climate improved.

By about 7000 BC, early in the Mesolithic (Middle Stone Age) period, conditions were at their best, slightly warmer than today. The sea level had begun to rise as the ice-sheets melted, cutting Britain off from Europe and the Isle of Wight from the mainland. The hunting communities on this new offshore Britain exploited the local flint to make simple blades, producing a sharp cutting edge by knocking off minute flakes. Bone tools and barbed harpoons were also made – with infinite patience – and used in the hunting of wild horses, deer and reindeer. From their base camps, such as the one on Hengistbury Head near Bournemouth, they could anticipate the migrations of these animals in spring and autumn, could explore the valleys of the Stour and the Avon, and replenish their supplies of raw materials from the abundant flint in the gravels there.

The improved climate and the formation of thick brown soils over the chalklands encouraged the advance of the forests; gradually man had to adapt and discover new sources of food. As technology advanced, flint tools became smaller and more delicate. Tiny 'microliths' were favoured by the peoples of the Mesolithic period to tip their arrows, or were used in numbers to barb spears and form the cutting edges of saws and graters; cruder flint scrapers were made for the preparation of animal carcases. Hunting was still the most important activity but now it was more systematic; for instance, study of the bone débris left behind shows that it was the deer stags that were culled rather than the hinds or calves. Similarly, the quantities of ivy pollen found in excavations on Winfrith Heath in southern Dorset, suggest that some of the forest animals were kept in herds and fed on ivy during the winter months. All along the coast of Wessex, Mesolithic artefacts have been discovered. Excavations near Corfe Castle and on the Isle of Portland have illustrated how Mesolithic hunters could also make the most of the riches of the seashore, leaving behind the shells of limpets and winkles in their rubbish dumps.

An additional attraction of Portland was the chert – a flint-like rock – to be found there. Excellent for making microliths, this distinctive material was traded by these mobile hunting bands over the whole area to the west of a line joining Brighton and Bristol. The traffic was not all one way, for blades of slate from Devon and Cornwall were reaching Hampshire about 6000 BC. Inland, the surface deposits of clay-with-flints could be exploited at Pentridge and Iwerne Courtney in Dorset, while at Downton to the south of Salisbury flimsy huts or shelters seem to have been erected on a gravel terrace above the River Avon. (The recurring basic needs of human settlement are well illustrated at this site, which was also occupied in the succeeding Neolithic and Bronze Ages, later by a Norman castle, and now by a modern housing estate.) A slightly more substantial structure, sturdy enough to be a winter home rather than just a summer shelter, has been excavated at Braishfield near Romsey. One of only about half a dozen contemporary domestic sites known in England, Braishfield produced nearly 100,000 struck flints. This extraordinary total is put in perspective by the length of occupation on the site, from about

Hengistbury Head, rearing up between the sea and Christchurch Harbour (upper right), was the site of Paleolithic and Mesolithic settlements and still contains over a dozen Bronze Age barrows. The double dykes across the neck of the heathland peninsula turned it into a huge hill fort that became a cross-Channel port in the late Iron Age.

7000–5000 BC, a time span similar to that dividing us from the birth of Christ.

The small communities that lived in these settlements very gradually began to take the upper hand in the search for food; no longer simply dependent on Nature in his hunting and gathering of forest fruits, man started to shape his own environment. Pollen, preserved in datable bogland deposits, tells us that the forests were being slowly cleared: animals such as wild cattle and deer could be encouraged to graze and fatten in the clearings and there are signs of plants like buckthorn which thrives in areas of cultivation. This was the beginning of the first great revolution in British history: the introduction of agriculture.

WEALTH FROM THE LAND

Into this simple but harsh world of hunters and gatherers came boatloads of pioneers from the continent, obeying the call to adventure in new lands. Probably arriving late in summer, after harvest, they brought with them seedcorn for their wheat and barley, and domesticated strains of cattle and sheep. There must have been many settlers, or many natives eager to imitate their ways, for their Neolithic (New Stone Age) cultures spread rapidly throughout Britain. It is highly likely that some of these colonists landed on the coast of Wessex since this now rapidly became an area of great importance.

By about 4200 BC they had already begun to raise the monuments to their dead. These are the famous long barrows, tapering mounds 100–200 ft (30–60 m) in length, built from the chalk thrown up from parallel side-ditches. The vast majority of these beautiful grass-green mounds – like whales surfacing for a moment in a placid sea – are on the Wessex downlands. Many have been levelled by ploughing but fine examples are still to be seen: White Barrow near Tilshead; at the Winterbourne Stoke roundabout close to Stonehenge; on White Sheet Hill near Ansty in the Vale of Wardour; at Pimperne outside Blandford; on Nine Barrow Down between Corfe and Swanage; on Thickthorn Down in Cranborne Chase, and the 'Duck's Nest' barrow near Rockbourne.

It has been estimated that some of these barrows would have taken half a dozen men as much as four months to build. Thus although the very first settlers would have been wholly concerned with establishing themselves, society must rapidly have become highly organized and capable of working together on such projects. The barrows were evidently meant to be *seen;* they were often sited on prominent ridges and may have acted as territorial symbols in the newly cleared forest. Their primary function, however, was as communal burial-places. Up to fifty skeletons have been found beneath the higher and broader eastern ends of the mounds, although the average number was about six. From their fragmentary and disarticulated state, with long bones and skulls sometimes stacked in piles, it seems that the corpses were exposed to the rough mercies of the carrion crows until a barrow could be built for them.

Only the privileged few can have been accorded such pomp. If they were the chieftains, then perhaps some of the concentrations of these long barrows represent forgotten tribal-groupings: on the Ridgeway near Weymouth, in Cranborne Chase, and around Stonehenge. Another of these clusters, of particular interest, is the handful of barrows around Avebury that contain stone burial-chambers of a type most commonly found in the Cotswolds and South Wales. The tomb known as Adam's Grave, perched on the chalk escarpment high above the Vale of Pewsey, has the most dramatic setting, but easily the most famous and impressive is the barrow at West Kennet. About 330 ft (100 m) long, this mound contains five small burial chambers which lead off a short passage behind a concave façade of large boulders; dry-stone walling, with slabs brought especially from near Bath, was used to complete the walls. At least forty-six skeletons were excavated, and we know that others had been taken in the seventeenth century to be ground down into a patent medicine! Some of the earlier ones had been tidied away, into stacks of long bones and skulls, to make room for new arrivals in the millennium that the tomb was in use. It is easy to forget that these skeletons were once people; it means more when we learn that most of the adults suffered from arthritis and many had *spina bifida*. When the last funeral rites were over, the tomb was filled with chalk and the entrance blocked by three massive sarsen slabs, still standing about 13 ft (4 m) high.

Even the West Kennet mound is dwarfed by the 'bank barrows' of southern Dorset, 'stretched' long barrows which at Came Wood near Broadmayne and on Martin's Down, Long Bredy, reach lengths of 600 ft (182 m) and 650 ft

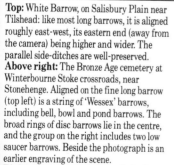

Top: White Barrow, on Salisbury Plain near Tilshead: like most long barrows, it is aligned roughly east-west, its eastern end (away from the camera) being higher and wider. The parallel side-ditches are well-preserved.

Above right: The Bronze Age cemetery at Winterbourne Stoke crossroads, near Stonehenge. Aligned on the fine long barrow (top left) is a string of 'Wessex' barrows, including bell, bowl and pond barrows. The broad rings of disc barrows lie in the centre, and the group on the right includes two low saucer barrows. Beside the photograph is an earlier engraving of the scene.

Right: The sarsen vaults beneath the West Kennet long barrow contained the remains of nearly fifty skeletons. The narrow access to one of the side-chambers is visible on the left.

(198 m) respectively. The poorly preserved example within the ramparts of Maiden Castle was over 1,640 ft (500 m) in length.

It is strange that excavations into long barrows on Thickthorn Down and near Avebury revealed no bones at all: evidently these were cenotaphs, but we do not fully understand why they were built. The mound itself was perhaps more important than the burials. Religious or social needs seem to have fuelled an obsession with long mounds. The most extreme form is the cursus: parallel banks and ditches about 330 ft (100 m) apart that run across country, oblivious to rolling topography. One such, 1¾ miles (3 km) long, is still visible to the north of Stonehenge, emphasizing that this area was somehow special long before the building of that extraordinary stone circle.

However, the most staggering example is in Dorset. This extends for 6 miles (10 km) from Thickthorn Down, near Gussage St Michael, to Martin Down near Pentridge. Long barrows lie close to each end and are incorporated in its course; although much of it is now ploughed flat, this cursus can be easily seen on Bottlebush Down near Sixpenny Handley. What were they used for? As usual the question is easier to ask than to answer. The long-standing explanation of them as processional ways may have to be rethought, since recent excavations elsewhere have revealed timber structures inside them. One day we may know.

The ground surface beneath one of the 'cenotaph' long barrows at South Street, Avebury, was scarred with the marks of the simple plough that had broken up the area for the very first time. The tiny snail shells found by the excavators suggested that this had once been mixed woodland but that arable land had given way to grazing by the time the barrow was built in about 3600 BC. The light soils of Wessex are

ideal for mixed farming and it seems that after an intensive period of cultivation there was a general move towards a greater use of pasture on the reclaimed woodland.

The economy and society of the first farmers may also be illustrated by their 'causewayed enclosures', the classic example of which is on Windmill Hill, just to the north-west of Avebury. This consists of three roughly concentric oval ditches, dug in short sections and interrupted by numerous causeways. The flat-bottomed and steep-sided ditches were quarries for an internal bank, although these banks are now often difficult to see; they were partly levelled in antiquity and have been abraded by later ploughing. Over forty of these causewayed enclosures, dating to about 3500 BC, are now known in southern England – nearly half of them in Wessex. Many are

visible only from the air as lusher growth in the crops sown above their buried ditches. Although up to four lines of ditches have been recorded on some sites, many of the Wessex examples have only a single circuit: Knap Hill, Pewsey; White Sheet, Stourton; Hambledon Hill near Blandford, and under the famous hill fort at Maiden Castle. Similarly, their overall size varies from a diameter of 1,200 ft (365 m) at Windmill Hill to less than half that on Knap Hill; perhaps their dimensions reflect the wealth and wishes of the community.

The function of these enclosures has been much discussed and there is probably no one single answer. The discovery in the ditches at Windmill Hill and White Sheet of food débris, pottery and tools, with the bank material pushed in unceremoniously on top, suggested a clean-up after a feast. This may have

The little Norman church at Knowlton occupies the centre of a Neolithic henge – the classic example of the superstitious consecration of a pagan ritual site. At least two other henges and a cemetery of 35 barrows lie round about, although almost all have been levelled by ploughing.

taken place during the autumn since many of the cattle bones were of young animals culled before the winter. The impression given is much like the economic, social and religious functions of a medieval cattle fair, for it is clear that traders brought stone axes from as far away as Cornwall, Wales and the Lake District, and pottery from Cornwall and Somerset. Complete cattle skeletons were also found, however, suggesting that stranger rituals took place. Excavations on Hambledon Hill reinforce this conclusion. Although large numbers of cattle also seem to have been present here, stone axes and other 'offerings' of antlers and rubbing-stones from near Exeter were deliberately buried in pits. More gruesome were the hundreds of corpses that appear to have been exposed within the enclosure. Perhaps a favoured few were removed

to be placed in the long barrows of the area, one fine example of which still exists within the adjacent Iron Age hill fort.

Whatever rituals went on inside, this causewayed ritual enclosure lay within a timber-faced rampart that took in the entire hilltop of 160 acres (64 hectares); it was 3 miles (5 km) long, required up to 30,000 substantial timber posts, and the entire defensive circuit must have made enormous inroads into the local woodlands. Such protection, reinforced with human skulls decorating the palisades, was not enough: the domestic enclosure on the

south-east spur was destroyed by a merciless assault that left many more skeletons on the hill.

The labour force needed for undertakings as massive as the construction of these enclosures must have been considerable even if, as seems likely, work took place over several seasons during the slack times of the agricultural year. A sizeable food surplus is essential if workers are to be taken away from the land for such specialized tasks. One labour-intensive industry was the mining of the best-quality flint. For this, shafts had to be sunk 10 ft (3 m) deep into the chalk, using antlers as picks and levers, and ox shoulder blades as shovels.

Two of these mines are known in Wessex: both are in the wild and entrancing, but quite inaccessible, landscape of Porton Down. A total area of about 50 acres (20 hectares) is peppered with the green dimples that mark the silted-up shafts; the mining has been dated by radiocarbon to 3100 BC. This mining process was more demanding than the collection of flints on the surface, but it was also more efficient. Complete production lines were established on site and the finished axes were dispatched for use in the local community and further afield. Altogether, society and the economy were moving rapidly forward in both complexity and sophistication.

The Wessex Henges

By about 3400 BC a new and uniquely British type of earthwork setting for community rituals appeared, apparently replacing the causewayed enclosures. This was the henge, an oval area bounded by a ditch with an outer bank. It is ironic that the name derives from Stonehenge, in many ways the least typical henge of all. More representative are the simple earthworks at Knowlton and, in its original form, Maumbury Rings in the suburbs of Dorchester. Each is about 330 ft (100 m) in diameter and

had a single entrance, although both sites have been modified since: the one surviving henge at Knowlton harboured a Norman church and Maumbury was converted first into a Roman amphitheatre and then into a Civil War gun emplacement! At a later date a second type of henge emerged: lemon-shaped with two opposed entrances. The puzzling ditch inside the Iron Age hill fort of Figsbury Rings, near Salisbury, may be an example of this second type. Its hilltop position is unusual but not unprecedented, for the three henges at Priddy, near Wells, are set high on the Mendip plateau.

The development of henges reached its zenith in Wessex, where the four largest ones were built: at Mount Pleasant on the eastern edge of Dorchester, Durrington Walls near Amesbury, Marden beside the infant River Avon in the Vale of Pewsey, and of course Avebury itself. Each has an overall diameter of more than 1,300 ft (400 m) and the biggest, Marden, covers an area of 50 acres (20 hectares). Stonehenge is not one of these huge Wessex henges; it is exceptional because of the stone circles built there in its later phases, but until then it was fairly run-of-the- mill.

By and large, henges are found in low-lying positions that offer no natural defences. This, and the fact that their banks are on the far side of their ditches, implies that they performed a ritual, social or economic function rather than a military one. It is intriguing that each of the largest henges is 'paired' with an earlier causewayed enclosure nearby: Mount Pleasant henge with Maiden Castle causewayed enclosure; Durrington Walls with Robin Hood's Ball; Marden with Knap Hill, and Avebury with Windmill Hill.

The most thoroughly explored henge – and the most visited – is undoubtedly Stonehenge; it is also probably the most complex and least understood. Like the more familiar great churches and castles of later ages it developed over a long period of time, changing its outward appearance but retaining its special place in the hearts of the local population for over 1,500 years. There are still many problems to be unravelled in its building history, but Stonehenge began as a simple (if not entirely typical) henge and only later became much more complex.

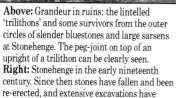

Above: Grandeur in ruins: the lintelled
'trilithons' and some survivors from the outer
circles of slender bluestones and large sarsens
at Stonehenge. The peg-joint on top of an
upright of a trilithon can be clearly seen.
Right: Stonehenge in the early nineteenth
century. Since then stones have fallen and been
re-erected, and extensive excavations have
taken place.
Top right: The south-western entrance
through the single rampart of the hill fort of
Figsbury Rings. The outer ditch has silted up at
this point, but part of the strange inner ditch is
visible on the extreme left.
Above right: Stukeley's drawing shows the
slight extra defences to the north-east entrance
in the foreground and the strange ditches in the
interior that may be a Neolithic henge. Old
Sarum – the neighbouring hill fort – and
Salisbury lie in the distance.

In the centuries between about
2800 and 2300 BC a circular bank and
outer ditch were constructed, probably
with a timber building or setting of

posts in the centre. Fifty-six strange little pits – the 'Aubrey Holes' – were dug just inside the bank, only to be refilled with chalk almost at once. About 2150 BC the direction of the entrance was changed slightly, perhaps to coincide with the rising of the sun on Midsummer's Day over the outlying Heel Stone. Soon afterwards a double concentric circle or horseshoe of stones was set up in the centre; these were the famous 'bluestones', which are said to have been transported all the way from the Prescelly Mountains of South Wales. Apart from the origin of the bluestones, none of this was exceptional. The next stage, however, probably coincided with the exceptionally rich and ostentatious period known as the 'Wessex Culture'. In the centre of Stonehenge a lintelled circle of huge sarsen stones now surrounded a horseshoe arrangement of 'trilithons' – two freestanding uprights capped by a single lintel. The sarsens may have been dragged from as far away as the Marlborough Downs, but since these stones occur over a wider area of central Wiltshire it is impossible to prove their source precisely. The original earthworks of the henge were now largely irrelevant; the ditch had almost entirely silted up, so much so that the body of an archer could be buried in it at about this time. Quite why he died we cannot know, although we do know how: two arrows, possibly from his own quiver, were found lodged in his ribcage.

Further rearrangements of the bluestones – first as an innermost oval and then as a circle concentric to and just inside the outer lintelled sarsens – brought Stonehenge to the form in which we see it today. Although now ruinous, it is still awesome as a feat of passionately inspired engineering, a leviathan carefully created. Not content with rough-hewn faces, the inner sides of the sarsens have been lovingly smoothed by the masons; the uprights and the lintels they held together by tightly fitting mortice-and-tenon joints, in a unique petrified carpentry.

All generations respond to this master-craftsmanship; although we only have glimpses of prehistoric religion, the pull of Stonehenge was still strong as late as about 1100 BC. At that time, a thousand years after they were first laid out from the entrance as a processional way, the twin parallel banks and ditches known as the Avenue were extended to the River Avon at West Amesbury, a distance of 1½ miles (2.5km).

The sarsen joinery at Stonehenge is a reminder of the complex rings of holes, dug for upright posts, inside the great Wessex henges of Marden and Mount Pleasant, at Durrington Walls and Woodhenge nearby, at the Sanctuary near Avebury and perhaps at Stonehenge itself. Most of these appear in reconstructions as the foundations of large timber buildings, but they could equally well have been open to the sky, the tops of their posts linked by horizontal beams: Stonehenges in wood.

We do not know if such things ever existed within the great henge at Avebury, but their places were taken by two simple stone circles; the one to the north contained a central setting of sarsens and that to the south a line of standing stones. These, however, appear now as minor monuments in a great cathedral. Avebury is huge: the top of the vast external bank of the henge once stood about 50 ft (15m) above the bottom of the ditch, now partly silted up. Inside this, the largest stone circle in Europe was set up, consisting of 98 sarsen slabs dragged from the downs to the east. These weigh up to 60 tons, and it was an incredible achievement to stand each of them upright in their shallow sockets. Two hundred more stones were used in the Avenue linking Avebury with the Sanctuary on Overton Hill, 1½ miles (2.5km) away. The construction of Avebury must have taken millions of man-hours; with modern machinery it would be daunting, but to move 200,000 tons of chalk, using only antlers and wicker-baskets, appears

Inside the great outer bank and ditch of Avebury

about 98 huge sarsen stones were set up in a vast circle. Some of the best of them survive here in the south-western arc.

almost superhuman. Whatever drove them on was quite as potent as the force behind the bishop's masons building Salisbury Cathedral nearly four thousand years later.

With Stonehenge and Avebury as such exceptional examples, it is perhaps surprising that there are few other stone circles in Wessex. Partly this reflects the geology – anyone trying to set one up in a soft rock, like chalk, would have been a laughing-stock – although timber circles could have been more common than we know. The tiny circle called the Nine Stones at Winterbourne Abbas, near Dorchester, is well preserved but the only other one worth visiting is at Kingston Russell; the stones there now lie flat, but the delicate wooded folds of the Dorset countryside make the walk to the circle a delight.

There has been much argument over why these stone circles were built and what they were used for; the loudest voices have been raised in support of theories that they measured and predicted astronomical events. Such a belief requires that the complex mathematics involved should be devised and mastered by priests who really *wished* to know about the movements of the sun and of individual stars. Much of this is moonshine. Early agriculturalists would indeed be interested in midsummer and midwinter, although they hardly needed the bishops of the day to tell them about it. Certainly Stonehenge may be aligned on the midsummer sun but elsewhere the arguments have sometimes been carried to ridiculous lengths.

What strikes us now is the dominating need to build, although the detailed reasons have to be left to the imagination for they can never be truly known. A classic early example is Silbury Hill, the great artificial mound just to the south of Avebury. About a quarter of a million cubic metres of chalk, quarried from the surrounding ditch, was heaped up and kept in place, pyramid-like, by internal chalk-block walls and stepped drums of decreasing size. The top drum is still visible but the rest were smoothed down to produce a conical profile. Radiocarbon dating, and the bodies of flying ants found miraculously preserved in the innermost turf core, tell us that building started one July or August round about 2700 BC. However, no burial has ever been discovered and

The huge bulk of Silbury Hill, about 135 ft (40 m) high and containing some 9 million cu ft (250,000 m³) of quarried chalk, dominates the valley of the infant River Kennet. The Roman road from London to Bath is aligned on the Hill and makes a detour around its foot.

there are no other indications of why the mound was built. Your guess may be as good as anyone else's.

In considering the great communal monuments of Wessex we have jumped ahead of ourselves and one important development needs to be mentioned. This is the introduction, about 2750 BC, of 'Beaker' pottery. Elegant and unusually thin-walled, these vessels are profusely decorated with the impressed marks of twisted cord or with complex geometric designs created with small bird bones or twigs. This pottery was common throughout Western Europe and although it is found in domestic contexts, it is primarily associated with burials.

It was not only the ceramics that changed: the old practice of burying the rich and famous

communally in long barrows and chambered tombs began to go out of fashion, to be replaced by individual inhumations under round barrows. Greater care now seems to have been taken with the deceased. Although one Beaker-using individual was buried in a long barrow, already old, on Thickthorn Down in Dorset, the more normal ritual was for the corpse to be placed in a grave, crouched up on its side, foetus-like; usually the body was accompanied by a Beaker and covered by a barrow. In the light of this radical change of burial rite it used to be thought that there had been an invasion of 'Beaker Folk'. It was suggested that the old long-headed population, buried in the long barrows, suddenly succumbed to racially distinct round-headed foreigners who preferred round barrows. Unfortunately the anatomical evidence is by no means clear. It is equally likely that the distinctive objects associated with the Beaker period were all adopted quite peacefully, by much the same social and economic processes in which North American culture is now found throughout the Western world. In this way the late Neolithic slid gently into the early Bronze Age.

In fact it was copper, rather than bronze, that was introduced by the first metalworkers, in the form of small but heavy flat axes and triangular daggers. European ore was used for one such dagger from Roundway, near Devizes, while another from Winterslow, near Salisbury, had been made from Irish metal. Other distinctive Beaker objects, all commonly accompanying burials, include barbed flint arrowheads; stone wrist-guards used as protection against the lash of the bowstring; and buttons with bored V-shaped fastenings, made from jet or from shale found on the coast of Purbeck. Strangely enough, some of the stone battle-axes also found in Wessex were made from the same Prescelly bluestone as was chosen for Stonehenge. Perhaps there was magic in it.

Surprising though it may be, identifiable settlements from the Neolithic and Bronze Age periods are few and far between. In this, even rich and successful Wessex is no different from the rest of Britain; all the community effort seems to have gone into the large ceremonial and funerary monuments (Beaker-using people were probably responsible for the first circle of bluestones at Stonehenge) and the small farmsteads of the period were much less substantial. Scatters of Beaker pottery in the plough-soil have occasionally betrayed the presence of a settlement, but usually these sites are elusive and have been discovered only during the excavation of something quite different. For instance, the flint mines and axe-factory on Easton Down in the Porton Ranges continued in production; when the excavators began work they found nine shallow and irregular scoops, no more than about 10ft by 5ft (3m by 1.5m) across, around which were the stake-holes for a light tent or a domed shelter of bent-over withies. These were the workshops and houses of the miners and flint-knappers. Such discoveries are unlikely to be made more than once in a while.

The agricultural side of the economy also flourished. Barley, much better for the brewing of beer, now took over from wheat as the predominant cereal crop. Flax was also grown, as the impressions of many seeds on the base of a Beaker from Handley Down, in north Dorset, testify. We can only guess whether it was used as a cereal or for making textiles. Wessex was quick to benefit from the increasing number of links now being made with Europe. For example, fragments of lava from Niedermendig in the Rhineland have been found at Stonehenge, along the Avenue at Avebury, and at the Sanctuary on Overton Hill. This lava makes the very best querns (hand-mills for grinding grain) and evidently the inhabitants of Wessex could well afford such imports.

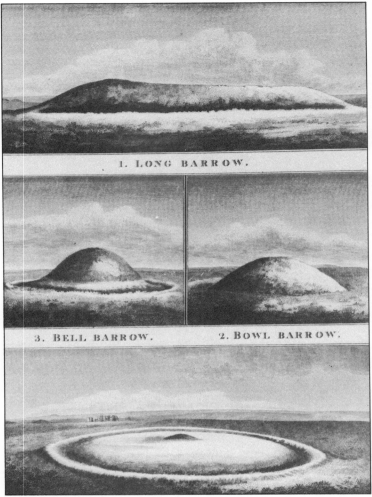

Above: A selection of barrow-types found in Wessex, as drawn in 1810 by Philip Crocker for the great Wiltshire archaeologist Sir Richard Colt Hoare, of Stourhead. At the bottom is a disc barrow, with Stonehenge visible in the background.

The Bronze Age Plutocracy

About 2000 BC Wessex entered what can only be described as an economic boom. It may have been generated by a change to lucrative pastoral farming on the rich downland sward; whatever the cause, the effects are unmistakeable. On the Marlborough Downs, Salisbury Plain, Cranborne Chase and the Dorset Ridgeway there emerged a flamboyantly wealthy and powerful aristocracy. Their appearance among the Beaker-using peoples of the area is so distinctive that archaeologists have christened the phenomenon the 'Wessex Culture'. Again, almost all the evidence comes from burials and thus has to be used with a little caution; after all, what we may be recording is not so much a change in economic and social conditions as a shift in beliefs and funerary ritual. Be that as it may, the changes were real enough.

The burial mounds previously favoured by the Beaker-users for their single graves had been relatively small, simple and shaped like inverted bowls surrounded by a

ditch. These continued in use, although they generally increased in size as they were joined by the more 'fancy' barrows so distinctive of Wessex. The principal types now devised include the so-called 'bell-barrows', 'disc-barrows', 'saucer-barrows' and 'pond-barrows'. Except the last, in which the burials were dug into a shallow depression surrounded by a low bank, all of these barrows are variations on the theme of a mound surrounded by a circular ditch and bank. Although these more elaborate barrows are best preserved on the chalk downlands, it must not be thought that the general range of barrows was confined to those areas alone. Barrows are distributed throughout Wessex, more profusely than anywhere else in Britain; indeed it is a surprise to see quite how many there are even on the poor heathlands of the New Forest. Evidently this was productive country to the Bronze Age farmer, even if we ourselves have not seen it in that light for a thousand years.

Some of the 'fancy' barrows have been found singly but most are grouped in clusters, as on Oakley Down near Sixpenny Handley, or strung out in a long linear cemetery. Particularly good examples of the latter can be seen aligned on the long barrow at Winterbourne Stoke cross-roads, just west of Stonehenge, on the bank barrow at Came Wood near Broadmayne, and on Bronkham Hill near the Hardy Monument. Indeed the whole Dorset Ridgeway sometimes seems to be one large linear cemetery, marked at each end by a bank barrow; the barrow-builders almost always preferred a prominent position, something readily provided by the 9-mile (15-km) ridge between Long Bredy and Came Wood.

The view from the Hardy Monument towards Martinstown and Dorchester, with two of the great chain of Bronze Age bowl barrows along the Dorset Ridgeway. Note how the vegetation changes as the gravel capping of Black Down gives way to chalk.

Some of the Wessex barrows are massive, up to 165 ft (50 m) in diameter and 16 ft (5 m) in height, indicating not only the high degree of social organization needed to raise them at all, but also the wealth of the deceased's family and friends. It was this wealth, expressed in a different way, which first attracted the attention of archaeologists, for the objects left to accompany the body in some of these barrows are remarkably rich. The most famous example is probably Bush Barrow, a bowl barrow still crowned with the bushes that gave it its name. Its position, at the western edge of the barrow group on Normanton Down to the west of Stonehenge, is unexceptional; however, when excavated in 1808 by one of the great Wiltshire archaeologists, William Cunnington, the contents of the barrow were found to be extraordinary.

The skeleton of a man lay on the old ground surface beneath the mound; beside him were three daggers of copper and bronze, each with a scabbard made of leather and wood. A bronze axe had been wrapped in cloth, and there were traces of a leather helmet by the skull. There was also an egg-shaped macehead made from a stone brought in from Devon and zig-zag bone mounts which must have graced something like a ceremonial wand. All this would have been quite enough to count as a rich burial, but there was more. The pommel of one dagger was decorated in a chevron pattern with thousands of minute pins of gold wire, each about 1–2 mm in length. On the man's chest was a lozenge-shaped sheet of thin gold, about 7 in (18 cm) across, which had evidently been mounted on wood or leather as the central decoration of some form of breast-plate. Another, much smaller, lozenge lay by his side. Both had had a geometrical pattern incised upon them by a skilful and delicate hand. A gold belt-hook, also with an incised pattern, completed the finery.

Who could merit such a grand burial? Evidently he was a warrior and a man of wealth and position, but the prehistoric world had no tombstones and even their princes remain anonymous. The burials of the Wessex Culture, the earlier half of which is exemplified by Bush Barrow, are unusual in that so many have been discovered. About one hundred are known, and they tell us that the Bronze Age plutocrats who disposed of their dead in this way continued to do so for perhaps as much as three hundred years, until about 1700 BC when cremation became the fashion. Even after this change the ashes of the men can still be identified by their daggers and battle-axes, and the women by their pendants, necklaces and beads. The disc-barrows, with their small central mound and wide outer ring, seem to have been especially favoured for female burials. To us they may only be exhibits in the excellent museums at Salisbury and Devizes, but these people were

Above and left: Bronze Age wealth: a fine necklace of exotic amber found with the ashes of a woman buried in a barrow at Upton Lovell in Wiltshire's Wylye Valley. Her other 'Wessex Culture' grave-goods included beads and other decorated goldwork, two pottery vessels and a dagger. Another barrow, at Wilsford near Amesbury, concealed the large 'food vessel' which also held a cremation.
Right: 'Celtic' fields near Abbotsbury in Dorset. Re-used in the medieval period, they fulfilled the same function as the strip-lynchets, providing arable land on sloping ground.

cherished by their mourners. In life, these nobles had taken care to beautify themselves, as the bone depilatory tweezers and the quantity of eyebrow hair in a Wessex Culture grave at Winterslow, near Salisbury, illustrate so graphically. No doubt they also laughed and sang, perhaps to the strange simple notes of a flute, like the one made from the leg-bone of a swan that accompanied a man buried at Wilsford, near Stonehenge.

Although the wealth of these people must not be exaggerated – the total weight of the gold ornaments found is small – nevertheless their lot was considerably better than that of the common people, of whom we know almost nothing. We can guess, however, that it was the wealth of the aristocrats that kept the others employed on grandiose building projects like the third phase of Stonehenge, with its sarsen and bluestone circles. What the workers thought of the schemes devised by

their masters can only be imagined. When these workers died, their graves would probably have been similar to those of their overlords, but without the attendant grave-goods or a barrow to mark the spot; thus the archaeologist often only finds these simple tombs by accident.

In this 'golden age', Wessex enjoyed trading contacts with Europe, at first with Brittany and then with other areas of northern France, with Switzerland and southern Germany. Some of the objects found in Wessex are almost identical to others found in the shaft-graves of Mycenaean Greece, and although scholars thought for some time that this trade was exclusively east-west, it now appears that Wessex may have been exporting to Greece.

Fields and Ranches

Gradually, however, the ostentatious wealth of Wessex began to fade and the community's resources appear to

have been increasingly channelled into maintaining and improving the fertility of the land. Now for the first time there appears to have been a system of wholesale 'landscape management' in operation, one carried out on such a scale that centralized tribal authority was evidently able to override the decisions of any one farming family or local community. The first manifestations of this are the so-called 'Celtic' fields (the old antiquarian name has persisted, but should not be taken as any indication of chronology or origins). These small rectangular fields, usually much less than 300 ft (90 m) across, were laid out in huge blocks, along alignments that often take little or no account of the topography. Cultivated with simple wooden ploughs, pulled first one way and then at right-angles, the fields that lay on sloping ground gradually began to accumulate soil along their downhill edges. The little scarps that this produced – a process which

continues to occur in modern agriculture – have preserved the 'Celtic' fields as landscape features.

Originally they covered all the Wessex chalklands in an intricate patchwork blanket, but having survived for three thousand years the majority have been flattened by the 'prairie-busting' ploughs of modern agriculture. Those that have been flattened exist as little more than a network of chalky lines visible from the air during the winter months. Nevertheless, some ancient fields survive in areas of old pasture: on Pertwood Down near Brixton Deverill; on Cockey Down above the London road leading out from Salisbury; amid later fields on Fyfield Down near Marlborough; on Wylye Down; on Burderop Down near the hill fort of Barbury Castle, close to Swindon; in the Valley of Stones near the Hardy Monument, and on the edge of the cliffs near Chaldon Herring.

Within these field systems there were small settlements of two or three timber houses; at first there was evidently no need for an enclosing bank, but small rectangular earthworks were later introduced. A number of these late Bronze Age settlements have been studied by excavation and fieldwork on the Marlborough Downs, in Cranborne Chase, and around Cerne Abbas in Dorset. One may still be seen on Martin Down to the south-west of Salisbury but otherwise they, like the 'Celtic' fields, have largely succumbed to the plough since the Second World War.

These settlements were certainly not confined to the chalklands alone: one enclosure on Beaulieu Heath may be contemporary, while occupation elsewhere in the New Forest is also indicated by the numerous 'boiling mounds'. Even if the houses of the inhabitants cannot be spotted, examples of these piles of burnt flints from their cooking places can be seen on Hale Purlieu, near Downton. The

settlements usually had a small cemetery close by, in which the cremated bones of the dead were deposited, with less pomp than their Wessex Culture predecessors went in for. Where they were used at all, the barrows are much smaller, but most frequently level cemeteries were used, the ashes being placed in simply decorated urns which had globular profiles or which were shaped like buckets or barrels.

These cemeteries are far less common on Salisbury Plain than in Cranborne Chase and the area towards the coast. This broad distinction is also true of the next system of landscape management initiated in the later Bronze Age: the Wessex linear ditch system. Although none has been found to the south and west of the line of Bokerley Dyke and Grim's Ditch (more or less the Dorset–Hampshire border), most of southern Wiltshire and western Hampshire was divided by long embanked ditches, or 'ranch boundaries': formidable barriers about 6 ft (2 m) deep and 10 ft (3 m) wide. Over 500 miles (800 km) of such boundaries have been traced in Hampshire alone. One of the best examples lies to the north-east of Salisbury, where there is a unified system of broad strip-like territories: each one crosses the Bourne Valley to take in both the flood-plain and the high downland – an equable division of resources that was also to be established in the parish boundaries of medieval Wessex. On Bulford Down a ranch boundary cuts cruelly across the little 'Celtic' fields as a deep and poorly healed scar.

The brutal introduction of this new form of land allotment must have been carried out by the contemporary equivalent of the National Farmers' Union or, perhaps more likely, was imposed by some central authority. Some of the ditches meet at suitable vantage points, one or two of which were subsequently taken over as the sites of hill forts; this is what happened at Whitsbury, between Salisbury and Fordingbridge,

while at Quarley, near Grateley, the ramparts can be seen lying right over the earlier boundaries.

It is evident that Wessex society had lost none of the cohesive strength that it had possessed since the early Neolithic period. Presumably this sudden rationalization indicates a wholesale switch to pastoral farming, although of course the arable was not abandoned altogether. The ranch boundaries immediately to the south of Woolbury hill fort neatly divide the pasture from the cultivated 'Celtic' fields to the north, and on Snail Down near Tidworth a ditch makes a sharp detour to keep the earlier Bronze Age barrow cemetery within the grazing. The graves of the ancestors could not be disturbed, even to help feed the living.

The ranch boundaries also strike a more sombre note – a consciousness of territory and of social tension. A defensive timber stockade had already been built on Ram's Hill on the Berkshire Downs well before 1000BC. That other early hilltop forts may have come into use is suggested by the fine late Bronze Age sword which turned up within the ramparts of the later hill fort of Figsbury Rings, near Salisbury; though the overall picture is sketchy, other early material is known from as far away as the forts of Chalbury, near Weymouth, and Bindon, near Lulworth.

An Age of Hill Forts

At long last, in the thousand years before the birth of Christ, the emphasis in the archaeological record shifts from the dead to the living. Indeed, apart from a small number of simple graves in southern Dorset and a handful of skeletons dumped rather unceremoniously into ditches and disused storage pits, we know almost nothing about local burial traditions. This is the Age of Hill Forts, when once again Wessex managed to become a sort of Iron Age Texas, building everything larger and more impressively than anywhere else.

Although it is the hill forts that survive to dominate the landscape, most of the population lived elsewhere. Fieldwork and aerial photography have revealed the large number of small undefended farmsteads that filled up the countryside. The most famous is the site at Little Woodbury, now a yellow sea of barley on the hill top close to Odstock Hospital, and within sight of the red-brick tentacles of suburban Salisbury. Here a single round thatched farmhouse was surrounded first by a stockade and then by a simple bank and ditch; in the farmyard there were small rectangular raised granaries and underground storage pits. The house at Little Woodbury was very large, about 45 ft (14 m) in diameter; a good idea of its spaciousness can be gained at the Ancient Farm demonstration area in Queen Elizabeth Forest Park, near Petersfield, where a house of a similar size has been reconstructed, using information gained from the excavation of a farmstead at Pimperne just outside Blandford.

A contemporary site at Gussage All Saints in Cranborne Chase, occupied from the fifth century BC until about the time of the Roman conquest, appears to have had a profitable side-line: the excavators found a large quantity of metal-working débris indicating that someone was specializing in the production of bronze horse harness. Both Little Woodbury and Gussage had antennae-like ditches leading away from their single entrances. In this they are similar to the 'banjo' enclosures of Hampshire, circular enclosures with long funnelled entrance-trackways, presumably designed to control the movement of livestock, which continued in use from about the third century BC into the Roman period.

Most of the small settlements have fallen victim to the plough and the most obvious features of the surviving Iron Age landscape

'Celtic' fields at Black Down Barn in the Valley of Stones near Littlebredy in Dorset. The sarsens in the valley bottom have been cleared off these fields, which are bounded by low banks and scarps – all being the by-products of intensive cultivation.

An Iron Age house, from a farmstead excavated at Pimperne, near Blandford Forum, and reconstructed in the Queeen Elizabeth Forest Park outside Petersfield in Hampshire. The reconstruction required over 200 trees, four tons of thatch and ten tons of daub to plaster the walls. Haystacks, stock-pens and a covered storage-pit occupy the farmyard.

are the hill forts. The construction of such earthwork monsters must have put a strain on any economy or society but Wessex was up to it, building three times the English average of very large forts. Even these vary enormously in size: Walbury in the extreme south-west of Berkshire, Maiden Castle, Hambledon Hill, and St Catherine's Hill, Winchester, cover about 80, 47, 30 and 20 acres (33, 19, 12 and 9 hectares) respectively, while Buckland Rings near Lymington (8 acres/3 hectares) and Abbotsbury Castle on the Dorset coast (less than 5 acres/2 hectares) are at the other end of the range.

Natural defences were exploited wherever possible, with the ramparts following the contours; Hod Hill, near Blandford, and Cley Hill, Warminster, are good examples. The most economical method was to cut across the neck of a promontory; inland, a modest result was achieved in this way at White Sheet Castle, near Stourhead, but on the coast more ambitious projects were realized. At Hengistbury Head, on Christchurch Harbour, 175 acres (70 hectares) were enclosed, while above Lulworth Cove the fort of Bindon was more than half as large again, with a rampart over $1\frac{1}{2}$ miles (2.5 km) long. More usually, the

Left: Only one rampart was needed to defend the hill fort of Bratton Castle on its northern side, but on the gentler slopes two lines of defence were dug. The sanctity of the Neolithic long barrow inside the fort was respected by the Iron Age inhabitants. The white horse was re-cut in 1778.
Above: The fine hill fort on Beacon Hill, near Burghclere in north-west Hampshire. The interior has never been ploughed, so about twenty round houses can still be traced in the turf – an unusual survival for Wessex.

fort had to rely on the strength of its ramparts and ditches alone: Badbury Rings crowns a slight swelling in the chalk country near Wimborne, but Yarnbury, though on high ground at the edge of Salisbury Plain, appears to have no natural advantages at all. Buzbury, crossed by the Blandford–Wimborne road, is even less typical, being on the slope of the hill.

In general there seems to have been a progression from a single line of defence to multiple ramparts and ditches, and from a stockade to a wall and then a smooth rampart of earth and rubble, although this is certainly not true of all sites. Defences must have been built in depth as a response to increased tribal rivalries, but in many instances they also reflect the topography. At Bratton Castle, Westbury, the single northern rampart and ditch follow the crest of the down, whereas on the gentler gradients of the south side two ramparts were required. The weakest points were always the entrances and these were frequently refurbished: ten

phases of rebuilding have been discovered in the east gate of Danebury, near Stockbridge. Some forts, such as Quarley, had simple gated gaps, or were protected by small outer banks, as at Figsbury or Old Sarum; others, such as Maiden Castle and Danebury, eventually became almost labyrinthine in their complexity, forcing any attacker to present first one flank and then the other to the merciless fire of sling-shot from the defenders.

Where the interior of the fort has escaped the plough, shallow scoops and circular grooves betray the positions of wooden buildings. Over two hundred of these can be seen on Hambledon Hill; a similar number probably existed within the ramparts on Hod Hill across the valley, although only a third still survive. Huts can also be traced in the undisturbed turf on Beacon Hill, Burghclere, and at Cley Hill outside Warminster; houses and the shallow depressions marking the deep pits in which grain and other goods were stored are visible at

Chalbury, near Weymouth, while on Eggardon Hill, near Bridport, the whole interior is peppered with these pits. The excavations at Danebury have revealed the extraordinary complexity of one of these forts, with its circular houses, rectangular raised granaries, and storage pits, all carefully allocated their positions on each side of the central thoroughfare.

The forts were not static creations but expanded or contracted through time. Some, such as Yarnbury and Scratchbury, seem to have grown concentrically and wholly enclose the earlier site; others, such as Maiden Castle and Hambledon, began by enclosing one knoll and ended by taking in the whole hill top. At Maiden Castle this resulted in a change from single to multiple ramparts and an increase in the area from 14 to 47 acres (6 to 19 hectares).

A few other communities were less successful. On the edge of Andover the early fort of Balksbury, established as a contemporary of Danebury about 700BC, seems to have declined in importance from a settlement with large storage facilities to an ordinary farm. Over the river, the rather later fort on Bury Hill also suffered a reduction in size, as did the promontory site of Winkelbury on the downs of south-west Wiltshire. The latter has an intermediate phase that was never finished, the partly-dug ditches and ragged ramparts being very clear. Similarly on Ladle Hill, beside Watership Down in Hampshire, the small trench marking the line of the intended ramparts can still be seen, together with some rather half-hearted and disjointed gangwork in digging the ditches. The project was evidently abandoned at an early stage, but why we cannot know.

It has been suggested that some of the hill forts on the Hampshire chalklands, such as Danebury, were able to thrive to such an extent that they became the busy economic and social centres for a 'territory' of about 40 square miles (100 km²). Such changing fortunes may also explain the puzzling proximity in Wiltshire of such potentially rival neighbours as Battlesbury and Scratchbury, near Warminster, or Hambledon and Hod in Dorset. Another fascinating possibility is suggested by the appearance of some regional differences towards the end of the Iron Age: could these be related to the tribes known to us through classical authors? Northern Hampshire was in the territory of the Atrebates but the western half of the county and central Wiltshire belonged to the Belgae; in the last century BC the dominant hill forts in these two areas seem to have been abandoned and attention transferred to what were to become the Romanized tribal capitals: Silchester and Winchester. To the west of the River Avon and south of the Nadder was the land of the Durotriges, a people who had retained and continued to develop their hill forts right up to the Roman Conquest. For this they were to pay a high price.

A wind of change was blowing over central southern England in the last century BC. In addition to agriculture, some increasingly specialized industries – the production of salt, pottery and of objects carved from shale – provided a firm basis for the economic future. Hengistbury Head on Christchurch Harbour became a major centre for the import and distribution of French pottery and Mediterranean amphorae. Such sophisticated tastes are essentially a part of urban life; indeed a town had developed here, complete with its own mint. The coins produced bear simple inscriptions, implying that literacy had arrived. Prehistory in Wessex could not have lasted much longer. The rough shock of the Roman invasion meant that the birth of History was induced and premature, coming with a scream of pain but with the certainty of life renewed.

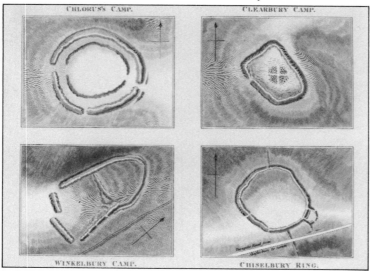

By the end of the Iron Age many hill forts outside Dorset may already have been abandoned. Sir Richard Colt Hoare published plans of some forts in South Wiltshire. 'Chlorus's Camp' is an old name for Figsbury Rings; Winkelbury remains partly unfinished and at Chiselbury single ditches and banks run away from the fort to bar the narrow ridge-top route. The clump of trees inside Clearbury, still a prominent landmark, was planted as an eye-catcher for the mansion (now demolished) at Barford near Downton.

ROMAN WESSEX

Harsh though it was, the military phase of the Roman occupation of Britain passed quickly enough. The effects of the invasion were, nevertheless, to reverberate through the Wessex landscape long after the troops had marched away for the last time.

The Roman forces landed on the coast of Kent and Sussex in the high summer of AD 43, moving rapidly north and west. There was some fierce fighting before the Emperor Claudius could be summoned from Rome to lead his men triumphantly into the native capital of Colchester, but the greatest resistance in the south was experienced in Wessex. The Durotriges of Dorset were probably not yet at peace even with themselves; unlike the Belgae of Hampshire they had retained their hill forts, which they must have considered impregnable. The Romans, however, were not daunted. The biographer of

The hill fort of Spetisbury Rings, set on a spur overlooking the Stour Valley. In 1857 the new railway cut through part of the fort's ditch revealing a mass grave: this suggested that resistance here to the Roman invasion was mercilessly crushed.

the future Emperor Vespasian – at this time a commander of the Second Legion – recorded somewhat laconically that in the invasion of Britain Vespasian fought thirty battles, conquered two powerful tribes and captured more than twenty hill forts, together with the Isle of Wight.

One of these unfortunate tribes was almost certainly the Durotriges. Three of their hill forts are known to have been besieged and some of the defenders mercilessly butchered; even the massive

earthworks of Maiden Castle were not proof against Rome's anger at being opposed. Those who survived the assault there buried the mutilated corpses of their kith and kin in a hastily-dug war cemetery at the east gate of the fort. The tribesmen had not had time to defend themselves with more than a fraction of the 50,000 sling-stones that they had collected from Chesil beach, over 6 miles (10 km) away.

Neither was any pity shown at Spetisbury Rings, near Blandford, where more than a hundred bodies were thrown into the ditch of the hill fort. A few miles to the north-west the defenders of Hod Hill were subjected to the murderously accurate fire of Roman artillery. Surrender must have come quickly but at Hod the Romans felt sufficiently unsure of their position to take the unusual step of planting one of their garrisons in a specially constructed fort within the ramparts of the native stronghold. Apart from the earthworks at Hod, very few of the Roman forts built in the first phase of the invasion have been identified; however, we know that Hod and two others – one in the Stour Valley at Wimborne and another just up-river at Shapwick – belong to this traumatic period. They were occupied for the best part of twenty years before it was thought safe to redeploy the troops elsewhere.

Towns: the Civilized Existence

It was never Rome's intention that Britain should be permanently garrisoned. Roman civilization was not based on forts and the army, but on towns and the social and economic life of cities. Thus the troops that seem to have been garrisoned at Dorchester were soon transferred; in their place a new urban centre was established to act as a focus for the dissemination of Roman culture throughout the area. Many of the original inhabitants will have been drawn down from the slighted ramparts of their old tribal capital of Maiden Castle, just outside the town. The area that was built up in Roman times has continued as the centre of the town ever since, and for that reason few of the public buildings and facilities normal in an administrative centre of this size have been excavated. There would have been local government offices, a market place, public baths and temples; only the amphitheatre is visible today. Known as Maumbury Rings, this was carved out of a Neolithic henge and

Top: A vertical air photograph of Hod Hill, showing the later Roman fort, built in about AD 44, inside the north-west corner of the hillfort. The slight earthworks of the 200 Iron Age houses have been ploughed flat, except in the south-east angle. The darker spots betray the positions of deep storage pits
Above: The mighty defences of Maiden Castle were proof against native attack but the entrances at each end, despite their complexity, were weak points that the Roman legions could exploit.

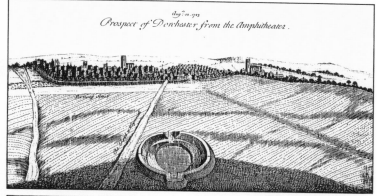

Top: Dorchester was still enclosed by its Roman walls in 1723. Maumbury Rings, in the foreground, was by turns a Neolithic henge, a Roman amphitheatre and a Civil War gun-emplacement.
Centre: The Roman road from Bath to London turning to the left to follow the contours along the side of Morgan's Hill, north of Devizes. The Saxon boundary, Wansdyke, used the line of the road but here deviates to continue eastwards over the horizon.
Above: Badbury Rings became a road-junction in Roman times. The road to Dorchester crosses from centre left to centre bottom.

staged productions ranging from slapstick comedy and 'music hall' to expensive gladiatorial contests.

On the more serious side, the status, wealth and civilized amenities of Dorchester in the second century AD can be gauged by the provision of an aqueduct 12 miles (20 km) long, that ran along the south side of the Frome Valley; it is best seen a short distance outside the town by the mouth of the railway tunnel at Poundbury. Similarly, it was probably civic prestige more than insecurity that prompted the building of the first of the town's defences in the mid second century; but about AD 300, with growing threats from outside the province, the citizens were in earnest when they faced the original earthen bank with a stone wall. Reassured, the wealthier inhabitants could build comfortable town houses like the one still to be seen behind the council offices in Colliton Park, which had mosaic floors, partial central heating and glass in the windows.

On the edge of our area, Silchester and Winchester had expanded from their pre-Roman origins as tribal centres to become sizeable and sophisticated towns; elsewhere urban development was limited to small market towns of local rather than regional importance. Of these, Mildenhall near Marlborough was at least graced with a substantial stone wall in the late fourth century when it became a base for local militia; the others (Andover, Wanborough outside Swindon, Sandy Lane near Calne, and settlements outside the hill forts of Old Sarum and Badbury Rings) grew up untidily around road junctions. These were comparatively *ad hoc* affairs, where local taxes could be collected and trade conducted.

Villas and Rural Life

Standing at the east gate of Old Sarum, the Roman roads to Silchester and Winchester stretch away into the distance. This is the visible legacy of the network originally designed to aid troop movements during the conquest period, but which was soon devoted to the development of the province's commerce. Good lengths of these roads can still be walked on the Grovely ridge between the Wylye and the Nadder, on Farley Mount to the west of Winchester and, most impressive of all, along the well-preserved route of Ackling Dyke across Cranborne Chase. Just north-east of Dorchester there is the rare sight of a Roman milestone which stands mute and ignored on the verge of the busy A35. These roads are almost proverbial in their preference for a straight line, but between Winchester and Mildenhall a most un-Roman curving detour, known as Chute Causeway, had to be made for $4\frac{1}{2}$ miles (7 km) to avoid a steep valley.

For many communities living away from the towns and the major roads, life during the Roman period continued much as before. Excavations in Cranborne Chase by General Pitt-Rivers, one of the nineteenth-century pioneers of modern archaeology, revealed that the farmstead at Rotherley, near Berwick St John, was occupied from the early first century to the late third century AD with few changes being made. The innovations amounted to the adoption of a rectangular house and the purchase of some better-quality pottery and furniture. As at Woodcutts nearby, which was also virtually unaltered until the late fourth century, simple agricultural improvements were taken up, such as corn-drying ovens; these improved efficiency, which was essential if the farmers were to meet their tax bills, most of which they paid in kind, in the form of grain.

The conservatism of the rural farmsteads from the late Iron Age into the Roman period recurs all over the area – in the settlements along the Grovely ridge and in areas as topographically diverse as Blackmoor Vale and Purbeck. Given a good site for his farm or his village, a

man must have compelling reasons before he will abandon it. This simple truth is crucial to landscape history and we shall return to it later.

In any age some have greater aspirations and opportunities than others. Even the farmer at Woodcutts eventually bettered himself to the extent of having painted plaster on his walls and a tiled roof over his head. Others had been ahead of him. In the generations after the Conquest it became the fashion to express status and success by owning a 'villa' – a Romanized house in the country. A simple mosaic floor, window-glass and central heating marked out the successful man. Plain rectangular cottages or aisled barn-like structures evolved into country houses befitting to the nobility. If you prospered you did not move house, you extended what you had. Thus a single row of rooms fronted by a veranda might have a suite of baths or a large dining room added in a complex, almost organic, way that often puzzles the modern visitor. For example, the villa at Rockbourne, near Fordingbridge, began as a round wooden hut but ended up as the grand focus of a wide court or farmyard, with workshops, barns and ancillary buildings ranged around it.

The great majority of these wealthy farms and country houses in Wessex have been found on the chalklands; of course there are exceptions like the clutch of three close together on the heavier soils in the Valley of the Dun between Salisbury and Romsey, or the rich establishment at Hinton St Mary which sits on a low limestone ridge amid the claylands of Blackmoor Vale. The best soils, like those around Andover, were eagerly exploited by a cluster of prosperous farms, but elsewhere there are large areas which appear to contain no villas at all. One of these causes little surprise for the windswept higher ground of Salisbury Plain has never supported a large population. More puzzling is the

absence of villas in Cranborne Chase, and it has been suggested that this was a vast Imperial estate. Within its boundaries the native farmers may have been kept to a subsistence level, all their profits being creamed off by Imperial agents to supply the army. There is no proof of this; nevertheless it may help to explain how, with the military in control of much of its economic hinterland, an important crossroads such as Old Sarum failed to develop into a town. The economies of the villas and the towns were mutually dependent, as producers and principal consumers. Elsewhere in Britain it was usual for successful villas to grow up close to their urban markets, but for some reason this does not happen in Wessex; only the north-western division of the Durotriges, centred on the town of Ilchester in Somerset, reached this final stage of economic development.

The heyday of the villas was in the fourth century, when rich profits were channelled into the adornment of the bricks-and-mortar of the Roman idyll. The most ostentatious owners – and there were many of them – went in for mosaic pavements in their principal rooms. Usually these were fairly simple but effective geometric designs, such as that from Downton, now in Salisbury Museum, but frequently they were richly elaborate scenes from mythology or literature. Probably the most famous is the portrait of Christ with the Apostles, from Hinton St Mary, their somewhat joyless faces framed by interlaced patterns and entwined spirals. At Littlecote, near Hungerford, a sumptuous mosaic is still to be seen on site; its interpretation is much debated, some saying that it shows Apollo and that it was the centre-piece of a grand dining room, others that the principal figure is Orpheus and that this was the focus of a cult-centre dedicated to him. Be that as it may, the mosaic may be admired simply for its beauty. Similarities in the designs of some of these floors have led to the

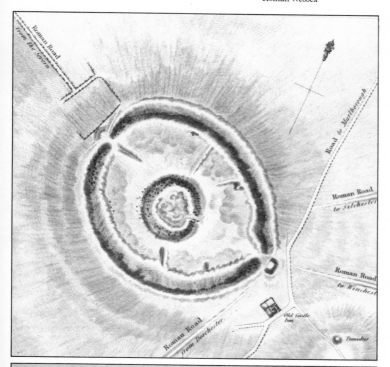

Top: Colt Hoare's plan of Old Sarum, emphasizing its importance as a junction for the Roman roads to Winchester, Silchester, Dorchester (via Badbury), and the Mendip lead-mines. The site of the Roman settlement here is uncertain but part of it was in the valley at Stratford-sub-Castle.
Above: The mosaic floor, now in Salisbury Museum, from the principal room of a villa at Downton. A large drinking-vessel, with dolphins for handles, occupies the central roundel. The tiny stone tiles are of six colours, and were quarried as far away as Somerset.

identification of 'schools' or firms of mosaicists, one centred on Dorchester and one somewhere near Winchester. Perhaps more than anything else the demand for these mosaics accurately reflects the wealth of the area in the fourth century.

Nothing, however, comes free and all this artistic indulgence was born of a buoyant economy. The corn-drying ovens so frequently found emphasize the importance of arable land, although the villas away from the towns and the main roads probably concentrated on cattle. By the late third century British woollen goods had achieved an excellent reputation for being hard-wearing and of good quality; as was to happen centuries later, many sheep must have been pastured on the Wessex downlands. Other natural resources were also exploited: millstones came from the Pen Pits near Stourhead, while limestone roofing slabs and 'marble' for architectural veneers were quarried in Purbeck, to be distributed throughout the length and breadth of Roman Britain. The potteries of Savernake and the New Forest were extremely successful, and those around Poole Harbour were quick to seize the initiative when a vast new market arrived in the shape of the Roman army. Along the coast that vital commodity, salt, was extracted from sea water; near Kimmeridge this was associated with the quarrying of a black bituminous shale which could be carved or turned on a lathe to produce ornate table legs, armlets or platters.

It is difficult to estimate just how much all this conspicuous Roman wealth and industrialization affected the ordinary countryman. Some, like the generations of farmers at Woodcutts, seemed to have been moved barely a jot. Without excavation it is also difficult to decide whether a particular site dates from the late Iron Age or the Roman period; the delightful farmstead at Ringmoor, near Turnworth, is an example of this. Elsewhere, hamlets of Romanized cottages were built at Studland, in Purbeck, and on Overton Down near Avebury. Whole new villages sprang up: on the edge of Salisbury Plain eighty platforms for rectangular houses are terraced into the gentle hillside at Chisenbury Warren, near Enford. What makes them unusual is that they are not clustered higgledy-piggledy but are strung out for 2,000 ft (600 m) along a 'village street'. A similar village, though with a more elaborate road system, survives on Knook Down near Warminster. This, like Chisenbury and others, such as the delightful Meriden Down settlement near Winterbourne Houghton in Dorset, even has a small 'village green'. More significantly, the villagers of Chisenbury and the farmers on part of Overton Down broke up new downland, their oblong fields contrasting with the old 'Celtic' fields still in cultivation.

The overall impression gained is of a landscape which comes close to that of medieval England: indeed there are good grounds for thinking that the structure of our man-made countryside has its foundations in the Roman period, rather than being a Saxon development as was thought for so long. This seems to be especially true of Dorset where, in addition to significant amounts of occupation débris in towns such as Sherborne and Wareham, Roman buildings existed on the sites of the later churches of Wimborne Minster, Tarrant Crawford and Whitchurch Canonicorum. Were these and many other villages also established in Roman times? In Wiltshire, the fifth-century Anglo-Saxon burials usually lie close to the parish boundaries, suggesting that these land divisions had already been in existence for some time. One way or another, it seems that the structure of medieval and modern Wessex had already been determined. Once again, despite the occasional desertion and 'mobility' of some settlements, once a man has a good site for his farm or for his village,

he must have compelling reasons to abandon it.

The fourth-century countryside may have been prosperous, but bad times were just around the corner. Inflation, technological stagnation, Imperial usurpers, and marauders from overseas produced a chronic insecurity. Landowners retreated to the safety of the walled towns, leaving their fine villas in the hands of estate managers. No longer under the care of their owners, these proud country houses decayed. At Sparsholt, near Winchester, the farmyard continued in use but the buildings were derelict and some of their stone was taken away for use elsewhere; at Hemsworth, to the north of Badbury Rings, the lead piping was stolen from the bathhouse; at Dewlish, closer to Dorchester, hearths were built on the mosaic floors as a final indignity.

As the fabric of society

crumbled around them, men turned to their gods. Christianity had become popular since its official espousal in the early fourth century, as the hundreds of Christian graves from the Dorchester cemetery at Poundbury have shown. But the old deities had not been forgotten. Although his exact origins are in doubt, that defiant exponent of unadorned machismo, the Cerne Giant, may be a representation of the Roman god Hercules. More conventional devotions on the hill tops were expressed in the traditional Celtic-style square temples within the weathered ramparts of Maiden Castle and close to the cliff edge on Jordan Hill, overlooking Weymouth Bay.

With no divine deliverance in sight the inhabitants had to hedge their bets with more direct action. The town walls would be secure for a time but the countryside was vulnerable. The great defensive rampart on the Hampshire–Dorset border known as Bokerley Dyke had been built against an unknown threat about AD 320; it was refurbished about the time of the disastrously effective concerted Barbarian raids of AD 367, and again in about AD 409. By now, however, the British realized that they would get no more help from Rome: the long genesis of a Saxon England had already begun.

Top: The Iron Age and Romano-British landscape on Ringmoor, near Turnworth in Dorset. Tracks wind away between the rectangular fields cultivated by the owner of an oval farmstead. Today's parkland setting is one of the most delightul in prehistoric Wessex.

Above: The footings of the late Roman temple inside the ramparts of the hill fort at Maiden Castle, near Dorchester. The square central shrine was surrounded by a passage or a verandah, and the walls were covered with painted plaster.

Top: The Cerne Giant strides manfully across the downland, club in hand. The focus of many folk-tales, his origins are unknown, but he could be the Roman god Hercules. On the skyline is the Trendle, an earthwork in which the village maypole was erected.

Above: The late Roman boundary of Bokerley Dyke on the Hampshire-Dorset border, snaking eastwards from Martin Down towards Blagdon Hill. The straight cropmark of Grim's Ditch, probably Bronze Age in date, is seen on the right; beyond it, keen eyes will pick out the rectangular end of the Dorset Cursus, two long barrows and some round barrows.

AN ENGLISH KINGDOM

The vacuum left by the departure of a central Roman administration led to the formation of small kingdoms which gloried and suffered in sporadic but intense bouts of rivalry. This disintegration, from the Imperial to the parochial, meant that it was easy for a few thousand Saxons to take political control. Some had been invited in as mercenaries by the fearful British authorities but the build-up in Saxon numbers was slow; political control probably only passed out of British hands in the sixth century, the Saxons eventually displacing even the most basic possession of their uneasy hosts – their language.

Arthurian figure, although the exact location of the battle is in doubt: sites close to the hill fort of Liddington Castle, overlooking Swindon, or Badbury Rings near Wimborne have been suggested. Other battles at hill forts commanding routeways took place at Old Sarum and Barbury Castle in the 550s, confirming the archaeological indications that the defences of many Iron Age forts were briefly refurbished.

Another late sixth-century skirmish was at *Wodenesbeorg,* the fine Neolithic long barrow of Adam's Grave that stands high above the Vale of Pewsey. Here the old Ridgeway route from the north-east was blocked by the eastern section of Wansdyke, a huge bank and ditch, up to 90 ft (27 m) across and still remarkably impressive, that runs for nearly 12 miles (20 km) to the edge of Savernake Forest. Nevertheless, the Saxon advance into Gloucestershire and Somerset was soon complete; progress into Dorset, on the other hand, seems to have been held up by more British resistance. Bokerley Dyke was probably again brought into service, but a retreat may have been made to another line of defence: Combs Ditch, between Blandford and Winterborne Whitechurch.

In the seventh and eighth centuries political control in England veered from Northumbria to Mercia; it was not until the early years of the ninth century, under King Egbert, that the royal house of Wessex was able to break the stranglehold of Mercia and take control of all the lands south of the Thames. But by now the terrible Viking raids into the rich agricultural lands of England had already begun. As the century wore on the marauding armies became increasingly successful; it was only the victory gained by the great King Alfred at Edington, just east of Westbury, that brought some peace.

From its base in Winchester (which was, in effect, the capital of England until after the Norman Conquest) the Wessex royal

Left: Wansdyke ascending Tan Hill, south of Avebury. More recently a great downland sheep-fair was held here every August.
Above: The great bank and ditch of Wansdyke, seen just to the south of Marlborough, snaking from bottom left to centre right. This defensive boundary may have been built in the late sixth century to check the advance of the Saxons from the Thames Valley.

After the ordered predictability of Roman life and history the frayed strands of evidence for 'Dark Age' Wessex sometimes seem to be weaving quite separate pictures: the fascinating study of

early place-names is fraught with problems for the unwary, as is the interpretation of the major literary source, *The Anglo-Saxon Chronicle,* which, in turn, is sometimes at odds with the archaeological data. Nevertheless, an historical framework can be provided.

It seems that the gradual westward advance of Saxon settlement into a tattered Romano-British Wessex was only checked by the victory of the Britons at *Mons Badonicus* shortly before AD 500. Here they seem to have been led by an

Left: The statue of King Alfred (870–899) in Winchester, the capital of his Wessex kingdom. By his victory at Edington in 878, Alfred was able to turn back the Viking tide; it was his foresight that laid the foundations of a united England.

Above: The late medieval tomb in Malmesbury Abbey of the great King Athelstan (925–939). Leading campaigns from Wessex as far away as north-east Scotland, he achieved the goal of his grandfather Alfred, welding Saxon England into one kingdom.

line reached its zenith in the tenth century under Athelstan and Edgar, conquering the north and the far south-west, reforming the coinage and establishing a workable government machine. All this was to decline rapidly in the face of renewed Viking attacks in the late tenth century, culminating in the conquest of England by Cnut (Canute) in 1016. He had fought his way to control an empire that stretched from Cornwall to the Baltic, but a strong man was required to sustain it and it collapsed on the death of his son in 1042. The

Wessex royal dynasty was able to regain the throne but the incumbent, Edward the Confessor, had been brought up in the court of the Duke of Normandy, and during his reign it was the Normans, rather than the Anglo-Saxons, who were most to the fore.

The stage was set for Norman England, but we cannot leave Anglo-Saxon Wessex so quickly; it is not enough simply to mention the great affairs of state without looking at what was happening in the countryside. The picture is grossly imbalanced since, as with our knowledge of the Bronze Age, most of the archaeological evidence for the earlier, pagan Saxon period comes not from their settlements but from their burials. Most of these are inhumations rather than cremations, grouped in cemeteries and accompanied by their personal possessions: a spear or a shield with a man, and a work-box or jewellery with a woman. Few, if any, of the cemeteries have been totally excavated; most appear to be fairly small but some, like those of about AD 500 on the outskirts of Salisbury at Petersfinger and at the foot of Harnham Hill, are known to have contained about seventy graves. A few small Saxon barrows have also been found, and a much larger number of secondary burials in both round barrows and long barrows. Some of these individual burials were richly furnished: one woman interred in a long barrow at Roundway, outside Devizes, took with her a bronze-bound wooden bucket and a gold necklace

The quayside on the River Frome at Wareham. The Church of Lady St Mary, in the background, has a fifteenth-century tower and was largely rebuilt in the 1840s, but it was already in existence by AD 700 when Wareham was a busy cross-Channel port.

set with garnets. Despite the grave-goods, something not normally found in a Christian grave, she may have been a seventh-century convert.

Most of the cemeteries have been found on the chalklands, especially around Salisbury, for the early Saxons naturally had a preference for land that was already cultivated and productive. There are very few early Saxon burials known from Dorset, and the later graves in Wiltshire – especially those in the prehistoric barrows – are in the west of the county. This seems to support the theory of a gradual westward drift into Wessex, with settlement in Dorset coming rather later. The most favoured locations for the early pagan Saxon cemeteries were on the valley slopes, in positions close to modern settlements. Surely, then, it is reasonable to suppose that these settlements already existed; certainly the later Saxon land charters and the Domesday Book tell us that the land-holdings were almost entirely focussed on the river valleys. It is most likely that the arable ground was now there too – something that would account for the survival of so many of the earlier 'Celtic' fields on the chalk uplands.

Villages and Parish Boundaries

Where, then, did the early Saxons live? Only rarely have their distinctive small huts been found, with sunken floors or shallow cellars. Some sixth-century examples which turned up at Old Down Farm, near Andover, may represent the sort of makeshift farmstead or hamlet that was then going out of favour. A tighter-knit cluster of houses – the 'nucleated village' – was coming into being.

One problem about understanding this period has to do with the cultural transition from Romano-British to Saxon: should we expect much continuity between the two communities and cultures, or was there a fairly clean break?

A direct clue is to be seen in the Church of Lady St Mary at Wareham, which was first founded in the early years of the eighth century. Five Christian memorial inscriptions or tombstones were found when the nave of the church was rebuilt in the 1840s: dating from as late as about AD 800, they are distinctly British in form and content. Evidently the inhabitants of Wareham still thought of themselves as Roman-Britons, calling their children by British names and writing in Latin. Saxon culture was not yet dominant and the British language did not quickly disappear. Most persistent were the names given to topographical features, especially the rivers: Avon, Cerne, Frome, Iwerne, Kennet, Nadder, Stour, Tarrant and Wylye, all testify to this.

Furthermore, it seems that the ecclesiastical and social landscape of the later Saxon and medieval periods may have been established on a much earlier framework. Following the mission of St Augustine in 597 the conversion, or re-conversion, of England had progressed steadily. By 704 the see of Sherborne was

established, and although a full complement of community churches did not arrive until about the eleventh century the physical bounds of their parishes were established well beforehand. We can be reasonably sure of this because from the eighth century onwards a large series of surviving land-charters define and describe the boundaries of the Saxon agricultural estates in great detail. Detective work in the archives and in the field has traced the landmarks referred to in the charters and it is

clear that the Saxon estates frequently coincide with the medieval parishes or their subdivisions. Indeed the origin of parish lands lies beyond the eighth century: the pagan burials of the earliest Saxons in Wiltshire (and to a lesser extent in Hampshire also) are frequently found to be grouped along the boundaries which, therefore, must already have been familiar in the sixth and seventh centuries.

If this medieval parish structure was already present in the

pagan Saxon period, it may also have existed still further back in time, in the Roman period. Just as most of the fine Imperial roads continued in use, so the coincidence of many Romano-British settlements with their medieval successors – for instance, the Wiltshire villas at Cherhill, Downton, Netheravon and West Dean, besides the Dorset examples mentioned earlier – implies that the individual land-holdings remained more or less intact from the Roman period onwards. The buildings may have been forsaken (no Hampshire villas have positive evidence of occupation after the fourth century) but the farm boundaries changed little.

Very few Saxon villages remained on the chalkland spurs that had been favoured at the time of the Roman conquest: Ashmore, high in Cranborne Chase, was maintained by its large embanked pond and is the classic example of one that did. But the most typical layout of a parish in the valleys of the chalk, well seen along the Wiltshire Avon and the Bourne, is a long rectangular block, stretching up to the downland watershed from one or both banks of the river. In this way the medieval, Saxon and even the Roman farmers would have had the same ease of access to the river-meadows, to the arable on the gentle valley slopes, and to the high downland pastures.

A pond, something rare on the chalk uplands of Cranborne Chase, forms the centre of the village of Ashmore ('the pond with the ash-trees' in Domesday Book). Ducks may have dabbled in a settlement here since Roman times.

Towns and Early Churches

What, however, of the larger settlements, the towns which a prosperous countryside needed to trade its produce? Silchester probably did not survive the fifth century but at Winchester occupation was continuous, albeit humble, throughout the dark days of the early Saxon period. Southampton, on the other hand, mirrored the renewing prosperity of Wessex, emerging in the late seventh century and quickly growing larger (but less densely built-up) than its medieval successor.

More modest in scale, and the most readily comprehensible of the Saxon towns in Wessex, is Wareham. There were Iron Age and Roman settlements in this position of great natural strength between the Rivers Piddle and Frome, on the higher reaches of Poole Harbour. By the early eighth century this was already a prosperous cross-Channel port. The principal church of the town, dedicated to Lady St Mary, was drastically rebuilt in the 1840s, but the much smaller St Martin's Church still survives by the north gate. Although this is later in date, probably belonging to the early eleventh century, it still has the characteristic 'long and short' quoins at the angles of both nave and chancel. Wareham's distinction, however, lies in its well-preserved Saxon defences. A huge bank and ditch still surround the rectangular heart of the town and its original grid of streets, about 770 yd (700 m) square. These defences were thrown up by King Alfred in the late ninth century as one of a chain of fortresses around Wessex that could act as refuges against the Viking attacks. Stretching all along the south coast, and from Devon to the Thames, only the one at Wareham is at all well-preserved, although there are some less substantial remains at Cricklade and Wallingford in the Thames Valley.

The other Saxon structures still to be seen in Wessex are all ecclesiastical. Of the grandest churches, there are some fragments of the early cathedral inside Sherborne Abbey, and the outline of St Ethelwold's New Minster can be seen at Winchester. More surprising are the tombstones and cross-shaft at Ramsbury, near Hungerford, which are utterly Scandinavian in their richly carved designs. Now only a village, this was the centre of an episcopal see founded in AD 909. Rather more is visible of the 'minster' churches, each one the mother church of an extensive area served by a sort of 'team ministry' of priests. They were later to be replaced by single-priest parishes when that system was formalized in the tenth and eleventh centuries, but in many cases their parishes are still large. The imposing Norman Minster at Wimborne preserves some of the plan of its Saxon predecessor, but perhaps a better idea of a minster can be gained by visiting Breamore, near Fordingbridge. This is a Saxon church that has been surprisingly little altered. The south transept survives complete, the Germanic inscription over the arch ('Here the covenant is explained to you') jolting the visitor into the realization that this building has stood here for almost exactly a thousand years.

At Canford Magna, near Wimborne, the Anglo-Saxon nave survives as the chancel of the Norman church but elsewhere the only indications of the minsters are their large parishes and some place-names: Beaminster, Charminster, Iwerne Minster, Sturminster and Warminster. Anglo-Saxon churches were not all as grand as the minsters; like the simple rectangular houses lived in by the members of the congregation, their places of worship were at first built of timber and roofed with tiles of stone or clay, or with thatch or shingles. These wooden churches are rarely found – they are buried under their stone successors –

The Saxon 'minster' church at Breamore, near Fordingbridge. There have been some changes – notably the fourteenth-century chancel and some Norman doorways – but the church largely dates to about AD 1000.

although one possible example was excavated behind Porch House in Potterne, near Devizes.

Some of the smaller stone churches survive, at least in part. One of the most famous is St Lawrence's at Bradford-on-Avon, which before its rediscovery in 1856 had been converted into a school and a cottage; decorated with blind arches, its high but tiny nave, chancel and one surviving side-chapel seem to sit bolt upright. This is not, as the Victorians hoped, the church built by the poet St Aldhelm of Malmesbury in about AD 700; it almost certainly dates from about three hundred years later. No-one need be disappointed, however, for on the inside, high in the holy darkness above the narrow chancel arch, two carved angels lie floating. Reflecting in their finely-sculpted robes the richness of contemporary Wessex, they probably formed a part of a Rood, or crucifixion scene, like that in Romsey Abbey. A similar angel still hovers at Winterbourne Steepleton, near Dorchester.

Many communities – perhaps those that could not at first afford to build a full church – invested in a carved cross where the Gospel could be preached. There is a fine one at Todber near Gillingham, its sides encrusted with leaves and intertwined scrolls. The strange ninth-century sculpture of the dancing man in the church at Codford St Peter, in the Wylye Valley, may be part of another such cross.

Churches, crosses and villages: these are some of the familiar constituents of the medieval landscape and of our 'modern' countryside. The heady days of prehistoric and Saxon supremacy were over; Wessex after the Norman Conquest was in many ways a normal, unexceptional piece of England: attractive, intricate and ever-changing.

The tiny late-Saxon St Lawrence's Church at Bradford-on-Avon, showing the blank arches and imitation columns of the chancel.

CASTLES AND CLERICS, COUNTRYMEN AND TOWNSMEN

The defeat at Hastings in 1066 of the Anglo-Saxon King Harold by William, Duke of Normandy, was a political, ecclesiastical and social trauma which took a little time to percolate down and affect the life of the rural labourer. New baronies were granted and castles constructed in a landscape that has been documented for us (not altogether unambiguously) by the compilation of Domesday Book in 1086. In only one part of Wessex was there an almost immediate change: in the heathland of south-western Hampshire.

This was the core of the area set apart by William I as his New Forest, a royal hunting reserve that originally stretched from the River Avon to Southampton Water and from the Solent almost to Salisbury. Heather and gorse scrub predominated on the stony and often poorly-drained soils, with some true woodland to the west and south-east of Lyndhurst. Apart from a short-lived burst of activity in the Bronze Age, this wasteland had never supported anything but a modest population; the few small villages and scattered farmsteads around its edges, and on the better soils to the north and south of Lyndhurst, now formed obstacles to William's plan for his new enlarged reserve. Over thirty villages and hamlets were swept away and their inhabitants presumably resettled. So complete was the obliteration that the locations of about one-third of these settlements still

Despite an official attempt to exterminate them in 1851, some 1,500 deer still live in the old hunting reserve of the New Forest. Fallow deer are the commonest, but red and roe deer also thrive, together with relatively recent imports, the sika and muntjac.

have not been identified.

No doubt there was some satisfaction among the dispossessed when the Conqueror's son, William II, the detested Rufus, was killed while out hunting. The official account was that an arrow loosed by one of his nobles, Sir Walter Tyrrell, had glanced off the back of a stag, wounding Rufus fatally in the chest. In the scramble to claim the vacant throne for his brother, Henry I, there was little mourning for the dead king. It is ironic, therefore, that the traditional scene of the death of the reviled monarch, marked by the Rufus Stone near Cadnam, is now so popular.

But dispossession was not all. The Conqueror's harsh Forest Laws, which were not to be relaxed until 1217, valued deer above men: bows, arrows and traps were illegal and a poacher might face blinding or death. Not only did the king ensure that he would be unrivalled in the chase, he was to be unimpeded too; no enclosure of land was allowed, though in partial compensation the displaced commoners were permitted to graze their cattle, ponies and sheep in the Forest, just as they do today. The disputes that inevitably arose came up before the Court of Verderers, a body which still sits in Lyndhurst.

In the New Forest the king was sovereign, but at a local level elsewhere it might be the major landowner, be he baron or bishop, who held sway. The physical manifestation of this is the rash of castles built in the late eleventh and early twelfth centuries. As well as being the means by which a new aristocracy suppressed a foreign countryside, the early castles also served as a safeguard for the Normans against the natives. Later on the function of the smaller strongholds was less overtly political and strategic, as they became fortified hunting lodges and defensible manor houses.

In the first years after the Conquest the most effective weapon in the struggle of the few to control the

The Knightwood Oak, in the centre of the New Forest to the west of Lyndhurst, is one of the most ancient trees in the Forest. Timber such as this was to become the raw material for the shipbuilding at Buckler's Hard.

many was the motte. This was a steep-sided earthen mound, heaped up around the footings of a tower made of timber (and later of stone) to protect it from being undermined or breached with a battering ram. The overriding advantage of the motte was that it could be built and garrisoned by relatively small numbers of men. Ancillary buildings, like stores and a

chapel, were usually built next to the motte in the 'bailey', a semi-circular or oval area protected on the side away from the castle proper by a strong rampart and ditch. As the seat of the Anglo-Saxon royal house (London did not obtain complete and overall dominance in national affairs until the thirteenth century) it is hardly surprising that a motte was

Some of the most beautiful parts of the New Forest consist of beechwoods, like this one to the west of Lyndhurst, which are at their best in spring and autumn. Many suffered badly in the drought of 1976.

Scottish and Welsh Marches, Wessex is not an area that is immediately associated with castles, although ringworks here are fairly common and very powerful. The huge bulk of Merdon and of Ashley, close together to the west of Winchester, can be readily appreciated, although it is the ringwork at the centre of the re-used hill fort at Old Sarum which is now the most easily accessible. Two other monsters, at Devizes and 'The Moot' at Downton, have been radically altered, by later building and by early eighteenth-century landscape gardening respectively.

The great heyday of the Wessex castles was the anarchic civil war of succession fought out through the reign of Stephen in the second quarter of the twelfth century. Some operations, like the abortive siege by Stephen of the future Henry II in Malmesbury Castle in the winter of 1153, were central to the political stage. Others, however, illustrate the way in which neighbouring nobles took the chance to indulge in private factional warfare. One example arose from the efforts of the opportunist Henry of Blois, Bishop of Winchester and a brother of the king, who in 1138 built the great palace of Wolvesey close to his cathedral, and the ringworks at Merdon and Downton to protect two of his estates. Ten years later, during the civil war, Downton was captured by Patrick, Earl of Salisbury, who used it as a base to plunder the surrounding countryside; he was himself turned out of the castle shortly afterwards by the Bishop's nephew. Some of the smaller earthworks may have been thrown up specifically to besiege others: the little 'Rings' against mighty Corfe Castle nearby, and perhaps Castle Hill – now an idyllic site on the edge of the New Forest at Godshill – was garrisoned against Earl Patrick at Downton. One way or another most of the major castles, including Wareham, Christchurch, Devizes and Old Sarum, changed hands during these turbulent years.

built at Winchester within about a year of the Conquest. Although the most strategically important of the motte-and-bailey castles – those, for example, at Christchurch, Marlborough and Wareham – were adapted and incorporated into later fortifications, some simple early examples can still be seen at Sherrington in the Wylye Valley, at Cranborne, and at West Dean to the east of Salisbury.

The other major type of early Norman castle is the 'ringwork-and-bailey', in which the mound of the motte is replaced by an enclosing bank. This allowed the principal buildings to lie within the ringwork rather than on the more exposed summit of the motte. Unlike the

The ruins of Corfe Castle, which once guarded the principal gap through the chalk spine of Purbeck. Blown up at the end of a long siege in the Civil War, the castle dominated the little town at its foot.

Investment in the security offered by castle walls was an important safeguard. At the beginning of the thirteenth century, King John extensively rebuilt his castle at Corfe and by 1285 the fortifications had reached the final stage of their development. Favoured with some of the best natural defences in southern England, in the gap through the chalk spine of Purbeck, curtain walls and interval towers now protected the whole of the steep knoll on which the early keep and baileys had been constructed. Nor was it only the Crown which was prepared to spend money in this way. That other giant among the lords spiritual, Roger, Bishop of Salisbury, had been able to vie with Henry of Winchester in the strength and magnificence of his castles at Old Sarum and Sherborne during the Anarchy, and some of the thirteenth- and fourteenth-century barons were not modest when it came to fortifications. The castle at the end of Long Hill, Mere, was built in 1253 by Richard, Earl of Cornwall, with at least six towers.

The building of private castles came back into fashion in the

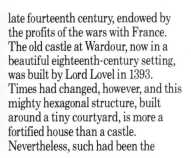

Top: The shattered shell of the castle of Old Wardour in Wiltshire. Built in 1393 and modernized in 1578, it was besieged and then blown up in the Civil War.
Above: The Iron Age hill fort of Old Sarum was re-used as the outworks of the great Norman ringwork castle in the centre, beyond which the footings of the early cathedral can be clearly seen. Gradually abandoned after the establishment of Salisbury in the 1220s, Old Sarum was one of the most celebrated of the 'rotten boroughs', electing MPs until 1832.

late fourteenth century, endowed by the profits of the wars with France. The old castle at Wardour, now in a beautiful eighteenth-century setting, was built by Lord Lovel in 1393. Times had changed, however, and this mighty hexagonal structure, built around a tiny courtyard, is more a fortified house than a castle. Nevertheless, such had been the

decline in the fortunes of the castles of Wiltshire that Wardour was very soon the only one still defensible. Elsewhere, Christchurch and Corfe remained in use, but Marlborough and Mere were abandoned. Old Sarum (to which we will return) had had little real chance of surviving once its town had moved away in the 1220s, and Ludgershall had declined in the

thirteenth century, first to a royal hunting lodge and then into a manor. This change to a less aggressive role is perhaps best shown by Cranborne Manor, the extraordinarily well-preserved hunting lodge built by King John in 1208. Encased in its early seventeenth-century successor, it is one of the best surviving examples of contemporary domestic architecture.

The Medieval Church

On a par with the power and influence of the secular kingdom was the medieval church. The bishop-barons of Salisbury and Winchester have already been mentioned but the monasteries were quite as important. Time has not treated some of the monastic buildings of Wessex kindly. Unpicking the plan of the thirteenth-century Augustinian priory from the eighteenth-century house at Mottisfont, near Romsey, presents the visitor with an enjoyable puzzle. At the contemporary Cistercian house at Beaulieu the fine refectory has been converted into the parish church and the mid fourteenth-century gate was incorporated into their new Palace House by the Victorian owners. There is even less to see at Shaftesbury, where the richest nunnery in England, founded by King Alfred, has been reduced to its footings.

Happily, the Reformation did not sweep everything away. The great churches of Winchester, Christchurch, Malmesbury and Milton Abbas, Romsey and Sherborne, are among the most glorious examples in England of man's hymn to his Maker. Largely built in the late eleventh and twelfth centuries, with reconstructions taking place in the fifteenth century, the buildings all have individual personalities. The solidly exquisite Norman arcading of Romsey and Malmesbury contrasts with the soaring fan vaults of Sherborne, with the reticulated tracery of Milton Abbas, and with the flying buttresses and delicate clerestorey of Christchurch. There is no room to do them justice here. Time is needed to absorb them, and silence.

Look for the people who built these wonders. Their faces can be seen in the Old Testament stories carved on the fourteenth-century reredos in the chancel at Christchurch, and on the capitals of the chancel aisles at Romsey, two of which are even signed by their carver,

Robertus. But perhaps it is the breathtaking sculpture of the south porch at Malmesbury where the medieval portraits are most vivid: disguised as Adam and Eve, as Noah, Samson, Abraham, and as the Apostles, they sit in their flowing robes and stare down endlessly on all who enter.

The churches were, of course, the centre of monastic life but the other buildings must not be forgotten. The cloisters and chapter house, refectory and dormitory where the nuns talked, ate and slept, are well preserved beside the sixteenth-century house at Lacock; but perhaps the most delightful, and most surprising, is the blend of the abbey buildings with the later house at Forde, close to the borders of Devon and Somerset. Here, in the last years before the Dissolution of the Monasteries, Abbot Chard built himself a great hall, fit for a prince, with a three-storeyed porch to match. More humble and approachable in its design is the thirteenth-century dormitory with its handsome and plain vaulted undercroft. The successful fusion of the ecclesiastical and the secular at Forde was partly the work of a later owner, Edmund Prideaux, in some ways an unlikely candidate for such architectural chemistry since as Attorney-General under Cromwell he might not have been expected to be sympathetic to things monastic.

The wealth that Abbot Chard and his counterparts spent to the glory of God (and sometimes to the glory and comfort of themselves) came from the extensive estates that were the financial life-blood of each monastery. The lands that went with them at the Dissolution formed the endowments of the large country houses that were to replace the monasteries. Their profitability before the Reformation can be gauged at their farms, often far away, out in the countryside, for it was the abbey barns, impressive monuments to the power of the medieval church, that

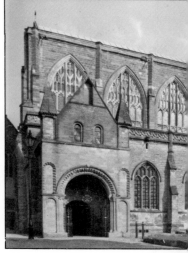

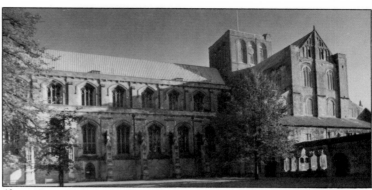

Above: The vast Norman bulk of Winchester Cathedral proclaims the wealth of a city that was once the capital of England. The lawns have replaced the cloisters demolished at the Dissolution, but the fine arcaded entrance to the Chapter House survives on the right.

Left: The sturdy Norman arcading of the chancel at Romsey Abbey. It was begun about 1120, in the same Chilmark stone as was used for Salisbury Cathedral. However, the architectural styles, separated by a century, could hardly be more different.

Bottom left: From the south, Sherborne Abbey looks almost entirely fifteenth-century, but it incorporates the remains of Saxon and later churches, as the Norman arches of the porch suggest.

Below: A double monastery – for monks and nuns, strictly separated – was established in Wimborne Minster about AD 700. The present church was begun before the Norman Conquest and continually enlarged until the mid fifteenth century, although the town it served remained small.

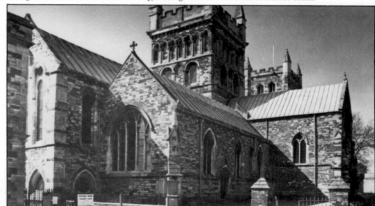

Above left: The south-west gate house of Sherborne Castle, the palace completed for the powerful Bishop Roger of Salisbury in 1135. Briefly owned by Sir Walter Raleigh, it was effectively destroyed after a 16-day siege in the Civil War.

Above right: The Conduit at Sherborne, built as a lavatory in the cloister of the Abbey, shortly before the Dissolution. The timber-framed house in the background is also sixteenth-century.

stored the annual harvest. There are good examples at Lacock, Bradford-on-Avon and at St Leonard's Grange, near Beaulieu, but the longest is at Abbotsbury on the Dorset coast. Despite its 23 heavily buttressed bays and length of over 270 ft (83 m), it still had a smaller capacity than another fifteenth-century barn at Place Farm, Tisbury, which is the largest in England. This forms the east side of an outer courtyard of a farm that helped to feed the rich nunnery at Shaftesbury. External and internal gate houses guard the way to the original house, the focus of a remarkably well-preserved medieval domestic scene. To come suddenly upon it, on the eastern edge of the little town, is to take a delightful step back in time.

The great barn at Cerne Abbas – still wearing a slightly surprised expression that someone should have converted part of it into a house in the eighteenth century – and the early brick example at West Dean were 'tithe barns'. They did not store the produce of a monastic estate, but took in the tenth part of the harvest of the parish – a form of local taxation which was used to maintain the church and to support priest and bishop. The surviving parish churches can also be good indicators of the wealth of a medieval community, and of its benefactors: an architectural barometer of their changing fortunes. Thus St Lawrence's at Downton, on the Salisbury Avon, is a large and imposing building, principally because it was a manor owned by the Bishops of Winchester. In contrast, the community supporting the small Saxon church at Little Somborne, near Stockbridge, could clearly afford to maintain the fabric throughout the Norman period and in the fourteenth century was prosperous enough to add a new chapel. (This is unusual, for there was little church-building in Hampshire around this time.) By the early sixteenth century, however, there was only a handful of taxpayers: the

The immense fourteenth-century barn at Barton Farm, near Bradford-on-Avon, that stored some of the wealth of Shaftesbury Abbey. The roof is covered with thousands of stone slates, and supported by gracefully sturdy carpentry.

chancel had to be reduced in size and the chapel was demolished. The settlement itself was probably destroyed to make way for a new park.

Among the parish churches of Wessex, everyone will have their personal favourites, and only a few can be mentioned here. Perhaps the best of the Norman churches are at Studland, across the Sandbanks ferry from Bournemouth, at Winterborne Tomson near Anderson, to the north-west of Bere Regis, and at Manningford Bruce, close to Pewsey. The first of these three is wonderfully complete: with its rib-vaulted tower and chancel and heavily-buttressed tower, it dates from not long after the Conquest. Like the more urban and worldly Norman Church of St John in Devizes, Studland is solid and robust: muscular Christianity in stone. The other two are much more modest: Manningford Bruce has a later tower

but its herringbone flint structure is little altered. Similarly, Winterborne Tomson is delightfully simple and endearingly unpretentious, with no obvious division between nave, chancel and apse. Later in date and rather more elaborate is the thirteenth-century church at Winterborne Whitechurch in Dorset, memorable for the strange stone foliage of its capitals and the rare shrine to the patron saint, St Wite. His bones were found in an inscribed lead box in 1900.

The fourteenth century, which was not a prosperous time for church-builders, produced some contrasts: battlemented Edington, at the foot of the downs near Westbury, looks rather more like a fortified manor house than a church, so different from the small tunnel-vaulted St Catherine's Chapel, above the end of Chesil Beach at Abbotsbury, which was built about the same time. In the fifteenth and sixteenth centuries the booming Wiltshire woollen industry paid for ornate and delicate structures such as those at Steeple Ashton, Lacock and Great Chalfield; at St Thomas's, Salisbury, where the roof of each aisle seems to float above the clear, plain glass of their huge windows, the light floods in, picking out the colours in the great mural of the Last Judgment that must have frightened so many parishioners.

The charming little church at Winterborne Tomson, hidden away close to Anderson near Bere Regis. Apart from the sixteenth-century windows the church is almost entirely Norman – note the narrow window on the left. The pristine interior is early eighteenth-century.

The wealth of wool turned to stone: Steeple Ashton Church, Wiltshire. The pinnacled south aisle was built by William Leucas, a clothier, in the late fifteenth century.

Out in the countryside the people and the land of the parish were the ultimate sources of ecclesiastical wealth. Although Domesday Book had recorded in 1086 how much tax the Conqueror could expect from his new kingdom, it was the *land* that was listed, not the settlements themselves. Excavations at the deserted villages of Holworth, near Owermoigne in Dorset, and Gomeldon in the Winterbournes, north-east of Salisbury, suggested that the earliest occupation there did not take place until as late as the twelfth century. Before that much of Wessex was still dotted with isolated farmsteads and small groups of cottages.

Villages and New Towns

The population of England at the time of Domesday has been estimated to have been as little as two million, compared with a maximum of about six million during the peak of prosperity in the late Roman period. However, the twelfth and thirteenth centuries were everywhere a time of great economic expansion, so much so that a recovery to around four million people may have occurred by the early fourteenth century. The effects of this enormous growth are still visible in Wessex. Although most of the open fields and the common grazings are barely recognizable because of their much later subdivision and enclosure, the pressure on the land can still be seen in the 'strip-lynchets' on the valley sides. Terracing into the hillsides in a series of long thin strips – like a strange staircase, wider than it was high – produced a useful amount of new arable land on ground that would otherwise have been too steep to plough. The most impressive strip-lynchets are at the end of the downs just to the east of Mere, but other fine examples exist at Coombe Bissett near Salisbury, at Woolland and Ibberton on the southern edge of Blackmoor Vale, and on the Dorset

coast at Abbotsbury, Portland and Worth Matravers in Purbeck.

The villages themselves grew in different ways. Many expanded organically from a single centre, but others grew up as an agglomeration of small units that eventually fused, like those at Bishopstone near Salisbury and Cheselbourne in Dorset. Elsewhere, some of the expansion was deliberately planned. Thus at Okeford Fitzpaine, in central Dorset, an extension to the late Saxon nucleus of the settlement was laid out in the twelfth or thirteenth century. The new development included a large green which, as time went on, was itself eventually built over. Such a buoyant economy meant that the grant of a market at Cerne Abbas in the thirteenth century required a new market place and the wholesale reorganization of the village centre. Even out in the unoccupied marginal

lands the effects were felt. Up on Fyfield Down near Avebury, a farmstead called Raddun was built in about 1200, complete with barns and newly broken-up fields; further south the edges of the ancient woods and heathlands were also being nibbled away by the clearances and enclosures of pioneering farmers. Even in the royal preserve of Blackmoor, licences were granted in 1314 for the cultivation of about 175 acres (70 hectares) of woodland in the parish of Hermitage alone. Isolated farmsteads and cottages were built, establishing a pattern that is still apparent in the heathlands of Dorset and Hampshire and on the edges of former forests like Chute to the north-west of Andover.

Of course, such innovators were taking a risk; for some it paid off, for others it did not. A general decline in agricultural returns in the late thirteenth and fourteenth centuries

Top: The fine series of strip-lynchets on the steep sides of the combes to the north-east of Mere. The area of arable land gained by terracing the hillsides in this way was considerable.
Above: Okeford Fitzpaine, on the edge of the Vale of Blackmoor, which illustrates the continual but forgotten growth of villages. The seventeenth- and eighteenth-century white cottages were built over a green that was part of an extension to the original village around the church.

by economic decline. Good examples of extensive earthworks marking the sites of ghost villages that had gradually succumbed in this sort of way can be seen at Winterborne Farringdon, just to the south of Dorchester, and at Yarnfield near Maiden Bradley.

None of these medieval villages was at all large by our standards, and in some areas it took a long time for prosperity to return. Even by the early sixteenth century Stockbridge and Lymington did not have more than a hundred taxpayers on their rolls. Ironically, these towns are both examples of another symptom of the earlier population boom, since they had each been deliberately founded and given the status and privileges of a borough by their noble landowners at the end of the twelfth century. These 'new towns', particularly common at this time, were an easy method by which the lord could increase his income from rents – in cash, with no risk or costs to himself.

The advantages for the new townspeople were that they had their own court to settle disputes, their own prices and standards for basic commodities such as bread, the rights to hold an annual fair and to levy tolls. Lymington, and another new town at Downton, near Salisbury, each had a simple plan: a new wide market place – still known as The Borough at Downton – leading away from the old settlement by the river. Hindon, between Shaftesbury and Warminster, was laid out from scratch in the early thirteenth century, and, like Downton, was carved from his scattered estates by the Bishop of Winchester. The long broad market-street had narrow plots running off at right-angles; so quickly were these taken up that the rents at Hindon doubled in the first ten years. Within a generation the town had over 150 houses, about the same as it was to have at the time of its eventual disenfranchisement as a parliamentary borough in 1832. By

may have been caused by a slight but crucial deterioration of the climate, by over-population, and by a reduced fertility of the arable land on the mismanaged marginal holdings. The Pestilence of 1348–49 (now known as the Black Death) which had entered England through the port of

Melcombe Regis (Weymouth) may have reduced the population by as much as a third, and Dorset was hit by another epidemic in 1381. Although perhaps not a major cause of wholesale desertion, these catastrophes were enough to kill off many settlements already weakened

Above: The Goathorn peninsula jutting out into Poole Harbour, with Brownsea Island and Poole itself in the distance. In the foreground is the intended site of Newton, a 'new town' planned in 1286, but which came to nothing.

Right: Constable's famous painting of the south front and the chapter house of Salisbury Cathedral, seen from the grounds of the Bishop's Palace. The artist often stayed at Leadenhall, in the Close, between 1811 and 1829.

the nineteenth century its origins were only betrayed by the strange fact that the parish church was still in neighbouring East Knoyle, from which the land that was to become Hindon had been detached six hundred years before.

The Rise of Salisbury

Most of the new towns of the early thirteenth century were modest in scale and have remained so; some failed and have all but disappeared. One, however, was extremely ambitious and enormously successful. Within 150 years it was ranked sixth amongst the towns of provincial England and may have reached as high as third place by the fifteenth

century. From the first it was the intention that the new Salisbury should be a cathedral city and the centre of a large diocese, although its genesis had been unpropitious. The settlement that had grown up beside the Iron Age hill fort of Old Sarum was for long overshadowed by nearby Wilton, which, until it was burnt by the Danes in 1003 was second in Wessex only to Winchester, and was the principal centre in the southern half of the county that bears its name. By the time of the Conquest the more readily defensible Old Sarum had acquired a mint and had become a centre for trade; it was considered important enough to be chosen as the site of the royal castle (the ringwork in the centre of the hill fort) which was in

use by 1070. Five years later the old diocese of Sherborne and Ramsbury was transferred there, and the first cathedral was consecrated in 1092, in the shadow of the castle. The proud and powerful Bishop Roger, who was also responsible for the castle at Devizes, partially rebuilt the cathedral in the early twelfth century, on more ambitious lines. Its footings can still be seen.

However, the proximity of such conflicting interests, military and ecclesiastical, was bound to cause friction, and in 1215 the Constable of the castle is said to have closed the gates in the faces of the clergy returning from a Rogationtide procession. Moreover, a hilltop site was simply inconvenient: water was a problem and the hill was so exposed that a tower of the first cathedral had been blown down only five days after its consecration. A valley site was required, but to transfer to Wilton would simply have presented the abbess there with all the rents and profits; new towns were in fashion, so a good commercial site was chosen, with plenty of room for expansion, close to the junction of the three river valleys, Avon, Nadder and Bourne. In 1220 a start was made on the focus of the new town, the Cathedral.

Only a building of great grace could overcome such a low-lying position so triumphantly: whether glimpsed from the edges of the Plain, or viewed close to, warm in summer sunlight or appearing to float, floodlit silver and gold, against a black and starlit sky. Its rare unity of design is due to the speed with which it was built, for within forty years it was more or less complete. The perfect example of the Early English architectural style, it is a confection of Wessex rock: the buff limestone of Chilmark quarried nearly 12 miles (20 km) away, and the dark, polished marble from Purbeck. The slender spire, at 404 ft (123 m) the tallest in England, was an afterthought, built in 1334 at some risk to the original structure.

To the north of the Cathedral Close, with its generous allocation of space to house the canons, a grid-iron of streets was laid out to incorporate the line of the road between the new city's older rivals, Winchester and Wilton. A supply of running water, led off from the Avon, ran down channels along principal streets. Development was rapid; by 1269 the population had risen so much that a new parish church, St Edmund's, was required.

The wealth of the parishioners, and of the city as a whole, rested on the backs of the sheep on Salisbury Plain. There may have been as many as 200,000 of them, reflecting the contraction of the arable land during the depression of the fourteenth century. More than enough for local consumption, the wool was at first sent away unprocessed: however, after the collapse of the Flemish industries in the fourteenth century the fleeces began to be traded, spun, woven and dyed in the city. As cloth they were exported as far away as the Mediterranean. Until the eighteenth century half the workforce was to be employed in textiles. The raw materials were close at hand, and there were ports at Christchurch, Poole and Lymington, but Salisbury also had the great advantage of being able to make use of new technology. This was the fulling mill for cleansing and thickening cloth; it required plenty of water power, but Salisbury had this in abundance. The contrast with Winchester was marked: no longer a royal centre, the old capital of Wessex was in decline. It maintained its riches only because of the wealth of its ecclesiastical see, although the city did benefit briefly from the wool trade in the early fifteenth century.

Out in the country, the rich clothiers were able to make themselves comfortable: men like Thomas Tropenell, who in the late fifteenth century built himself a perfect late medieval manor house at Great Chalfield near Bradford-on-

Top left: The cloisters, added as an afterthought to Salisbury Cathedral in about 1270. Since this was not a monastic cathedral, the cloisters were not strictly necessary.
Centre left: The houses in the close at Salisbury betray their medieval origins. Behind the elaborate porch of Hemingsby is a fine fifteenth-century hall. The little wing on the right is rather earlier, the multitude of herringbone tiles in its walls contrasting with the more familiar chequerwork of flint and stone.
Left: Salisbury from Harnham Hill in 1723, when the city had still not expanded beyond its original medieval limits. The spire next to the Cathedral is the bell-tower, demolished later in the eighteenth century. Old Sarum is on the far left.
Above: The exquisite medieval Westwood Manor, where the small house of about 1400 was enlarged in the fifteenth and sixteenth centuries.

Avon. For the comfort of his soul he also provided a fine chapel for the little church next door, approached through the gate house to the manor. Similarly at Westwood nearby, Thomas Horton had a new tower built on to the parish church and remodelled the manor house for his own use. Just to the east of Puddletown, in Dorset, Sir William Martyn could celebrate his success as Lord Mayor of London in 1493 by rebuilding Athelhampton Hall, a battlemented but utterly domestic structure now surrounded by an equally famous garden. Sir William's

Great Hall, with its elegant oriel window, fine open timber roof and original traceried door are of a quality that would earlier have been possible only for a bishop or a baron.

In its way this was a foretaste of the triumph of the secular under the Tudors. Perversely, it was also the beginning of the long move from the country to the town. Through the following centuries the working population would gradually congregate in the urban communities, while their masters began to experience the grace and comfort of the country house.

WAR, WORK AND ELEGANCE

It did not take long for the shock waves of the Reformation to be felt in Wessex, and some of the marks of those troubled times are still visible in the landscape. Relations between England and France were severely strained by Henry VIII's break with the Church in Rome, and the King knew that an invasion was a real possibility; to guard against this he built a string of new castles in 1538–40 to protect the harbours from Kent to Cornwall.

Along the coast of Wessex these were at Portland, Sandsfoot (Weymouth), Brownsea Island in Poole Harbour, Hurst Castle at the western end of the Solent, and Calshot at the mouth of Southampton Water. Quite unlike their more spacious medieval predecessors, these squat, geometrical blockhouses were really fortified gun-platforms. Portland and Hurst are especially well preserved, their fan-shaped batteries controlling the sea in front of them; of Sandsfoot only the garrison's quarters survive, and the remnants of Brownsea are incorporated into the basement of the eighteenth-century house.

Inland, Henry's measures were having a more profound effect. The Dissolution of the Monasteries brought about the disposal in the 1540s of the great monastic estates throughout the country. Crown servants and a rapidly rising upper middle class of prosperous merchants did particularly well, buying the land and (in most cases) converting the buildings into mansions fitting to their wealth, status and aspirations. Thus, the Cornishman John Tregonwell was able to use his position as one of His Majesty's Commissioners overseeing the surrender of the monasteries in Dorset to acquire Milton Abbey. The

Top: Portland Castle, completed for Henry VIII in 1540 at a cost of £4,965. In the late sixteenth century 6 gunners, 5 soldiers and 2 porters served there. It was converted into a house in the early nineteenth century. Portland is still operational as a naval base.
Above: The eighteenth-century Brownsea Castle, which conceals its predecessor, built by Henry VIII, in its basement. The castellated Family Pier, together with many of the other outbuildings, was added in the 1850s.

abbey became the parish church and the abbot's fine lodging was to be the home of the Tregonwells until 1752. Other Wessex monasteries – Abbotsbury, Beaulieu, Lacock, Longleat, Mottisfont and Wilton – all had to make this hurried transition from ecclesiastical to secular. One of the by-products of this upheaval was to accelerate the agricultural changes already in progress in the countryside.

An Enclosed Countryside

During the sixteenth century many yeoman farmers were able to buy their own land; as they rose socially and financially they were keen to try any innovations that might increase profitability. One crude measure of the change is the increase of the population in the succeeding century, from about $4\frac{1}{2}$ million to about 6 million, a boom which naturally created more demand for agricultural produce. The innovations that were gradually creeping in by the

Top left: The Old Manor House at Abbotsbury, in Dorset, was built of local limestone in the sixteenth century to a grander design than the thatched cottage on the far corner, which was put up a hundred years later. Reed for thatching is grown nearby.
Centre: Large portions of the medieval Augustinian nunnery survive within the Tudor mansion of Lacock Abbey, which was 'gothicized' in the 1750s.
Left: The nave of the Augustinian priory of Mottisfont Abbey still forms the skeleton of the eighteenth-century house: a perfect example of the adaptation from monastic to secular use.
Above: Avebury Manor, an Elizabethan house built on or close to the site of a small twelfth-century French priory. Set in delightful walled gardens, this was the home of Alexander Keiller, of the marmalade family, who carried out the major excavations of the Neolithic henge.

seventeenth century took the form of a more sophisticated use of rotation – allowing an arable field to 'rest' as pasture for a few years before being ploughed again – and the introduction of new strains of grasses, roots and clover. These better fodder crops boosted the nitrogen in the soil and improved the grazing; larger numbers of livestock could thus be kept. A related development was increased specialization, which in the sixteenth century was mainly concentrated on the production of wool. Hundreds of thousands of sheep now grazed the downs, and one farmer might own a flock of perhaps two thousand.

      With widespread change of ownership, it was inevitable that there should be a movement away from the old 'open field' system of agriculture with its long strips of evenly divided arable land and common pasture. Some redistribution had to take place. The usual procedure was for the landowners in a parish to agree how the ground should be divided; the new fields were then enclosed by quick-set hedges on low banks. John Aubrey, the Wiltshire antiquary and entertaining chronicler of seventeenth-century gossip, records how Captain Jones of Newton Tony, near Salisbury, sowed a single plough-furrow with the pulp of crab-apples 'which they gett at the verjuice mill'; the pips germinated into excellent hedges 'so thick that no boare can gett through them'. These enclosures were sometimes opposed by the tenants, who saw their rights of common grazing on the downs being taken away or who objected to the revised allocation and enclosure of the old strips. Occasionally agreement was not possible and as early as 1602 an Act of Parliament was required to sweep away the common fields of Radipole, near Weymouth. Such Acts, however, did not become commonplace until the late eighteenth century.

      The enclosure of the downland and the heaths produced

Salisbury from the air, with the Cathedral surrounded by the Close and the grid of the medieval streets beginning on the right. The valley floor between the two broad arms of the River Nadder is

large and distinctive rectangular fields, like those that can be seen from the chalk escarpment at Bratton Castle, near Westbury. The new fields contrasted markedly with the broad ridge-and-furrow of the open fields and with the *ad hoc* patchwork of fields that had resulted from the clearance of forest or gorse. Surviving documents tell us that these clearances continued in areas as diverse as the claylands of the Vale of Blackmoor and the downland and woods of Whiteparish near Romsey; new farmsteads were being built in scattered positions as the woods were cut down and the chalklands enclosed.

One problem that remained for the sheep farmers was the scarcity of good-quality grass in the early spring, before growth had begun on the downs. The solution – that enjoyed its heyday in the seventeenth century – was to 'drown' the riverside meadows. This sounds drastic, but if it was well controlled, the greatly increased amount of water meant that the grass could grow safe from frost until the stock was turned out on to these pastures between February and May. The usual method was to dig a system of artificial channels, dams and sluices; the water carried away from the river ran along the spines of low ridges that filled the meadows and looked very similar to the old ridge-and-furrow. The continuous flow of water raised the temperature of the meadow, allowing the grass to grow, while a complementary series of drains carried the water back to the river further downstream. Although almost all of these 'water-meadows' have now fallen into disuse, good examples can be seen in the valleys of the Rivers Frome and Piddle in Dorset, on either side of the Town Path linking Salisbury with Harnham, and a few miles away at Woodford. John Aubrey, who remembered when such improvements were introduced in the 1630s around his home at Broadchalke, records the wonder of

filled with the intricate channels of water-meadows. The Avon flows in from the top right, and on the left is Harnham, a village grown into a suburb.

the knot-grass growing in the water-meadows at Orcheston St Mary and Ebbesborne Wake in southern Wiltshire which reached a length of 18 ft (5.5 m); in the mid nineteenth century the meadow at Orcheston was still producing 5 tons of hay to the acre (12 tonnes per hectare).

All these new developments in the post-Reformation landscape came to fruition as the Industrial Revolution provided new equipment and fresh injections of capital. Between about 1750 and 1850 almost all the remaining common fields were surveyed, valued and redistributed. Acts of Parliament were commonly required for this in Wiltshire and in Hampshire, although in Dorset much of the enclosure had already taken place. On the Isle of Portland they failed to reach an agreement and so the common fields have survived. Some landowners were very enterprising: on Brownsea Island, Humphrey Sturt of Crichel reclaimed large areas of heathland, shipping in manure to improve the fertility. The project eventually failed, but the hedge-banks and narrow ridge-and-furrow cultivation can still be traced among the gorse bushes.

Battles and Building

Affairs of state usually made little impact on the lives of the countrymen; the major exception was the Civil War between King and Parliament. Some encounters, such as the battle in 1643 on Roundway Down, outside Devizes, were part of the central campaigns of the conflict; elsewhere, though the enmity could be intense, the consequences were less far-reaching. Even individual houses were involved: the manor at Great Chalfield managed to withstand a short Royalist siege, but in Dorset the fiercely Parliamentary town of Dorchester surrendered without a shot being fired – despite expensive fortifications that included the conversion of Maumbury Rings. The castle at Sherborne was eventually

Left: Kingston Lacy, built in 1665 by Sir Ralph Bankes to replace his father's home, Corfe Castle, destroyed in the Civil War. Extensive alterations were undertaken in 1835.
Above: The richly gilded and coffered ceiling of the Spanish Room at Kingston Lacy, said to have come from the Contarini Palace in Venice. The sixteenth-century paintings are from the studio of Veronese.

taken by Parliament, but at Corfe Lady Bankes held out for three years until the treacherous Colonel Pittman got a large party of Parliamentary soldiers into the castle under the pretence that they were Royalist reinforcements. Both of these castles were slighted so that they should never be defensible again. The same happened at Wardour, which Aubrey saw the day after it was blown up; it had been built so well 'that one of the little towers reclining on one side did hang together and not fall in peeces'.

By 1645 many of the men of Dorset had already had enough of the damage that was caused by the constant movements of the rival armies. Calling themselves the 'Clubmen' they banded together to protect their property. In one of the more bizarre episodes of the war Cromwell attacked and routed 2,000 of them camped in the Iron Age fort on Hambledon Hill near Blandford; 300 of them were held in the church at Shroton until they had given promises of good behaviour. Little wonder, perhaps, that the short-lived uprisings against Parliament led by Colonel John Penruddock of Compton Chamberlayne in 1655, and by the Duke of Monmouth who landed at

Lyme Regis thirty years later, failed to gain popular support.

Life went on, both for the grand and for the humble. It is fitting that, just as Forde Abbey had been remodelled by Cromwell's Attorney-General, so the Bankes family were able to build their fine early Neo-Classical mansion at Kingston Lacy in the 1660s – despite their reverses in the Civil War when Sir John Bankes had been Attorney-General to Charles I. Everywhere people were sick of fighting and wanted simply to be left in peace in their communities.

Many of the older houses in the villages of present-day Wessex date from the seventeenth and eighteenth centuries. Sometimes the use over a long period of local building materials seems to minimize the differences in style. Thus the Purbeck stone at Corfe Castle tends to conceal the fact that the houses there range in date from the sixteenth to the twentieth centuries; Morton's House in East Street speaks of some prosperity in the early seventeenth century, while the little Georgian Town Hall emphasizes the community's aspirations, and also its size. Further north, the rendered exteriors of the cottages in Milton

Abbas protect their thick walls made of 'cob' – a chalky mud mixed with straw, which was commonly used throughout the chalk country. In Hampshire, timber-framing is frequently found, as for instance in the village of Rockbourne where a long straggle of houses lines the road beside the stream. Under thatched roofs, the whitewashed walls and dark timbers blend with warm red brick, with hollyhocks, roses and weeping willows. In Wiltshire the grey sandstone sarsens, the limestones of Chilmark and the black and white chequer of flint compete for attention. Towards Bath, the Corsham limestone was used extensively at Lacock, although some of the charm of the village arises from its diversity. After half a millennium of village building the abbey barn rubs shoulders with the domed eighteenth-century lock-up; timber studding and Georgian brick, seventeenth-century and medieval doorways contrast with one another but do not clash.

In Lacock the village houses were modified or extended, demolished and replaced as time went by, in an almost organic process, and while all villages are artificial, some are more so than others. The most notorious example of this is Milton Abbas. At the Dissolution the abbey at Milton had been sold to the Tregonwells who retained the estate for over two hundred years. However, in 1752 it was bought by Joseph Damer, an MP and a local man who had had the good sense and good fortune to marry the daughter of the Duke of Dorset. Rude, proud and domineering, he ended up as Earl of

Top: Thatch, brick and timber-framing beside the stream at Rockbourne in south-western Hampshire.

Centre: Timber-framed Tudor cottages with attractive lattice windows at Hursley near Winchester. The projecting 'jetty' of the upper storey steadied the floor-joists and maximized the space available internally.

Right: The pleasing jumble of buildings and materials in the village of Lacock; the fourteenth-century barn on the right stored some of the produce of the Lacock Abbey estate.

Dorchester. At Milton he began to change the abbey buildings which had been little altered by the Tregonwells. Abbot Middleton's great hall of 1498 was incorporated into a new mansion designed by Sir William Chambers, and the abbey itself became Damer's fantastically grandiose private chapel. Everything else was swept away.

It was inevitable that Damer would resent the presence of the market town that had grown up outside the abbey; with over a hundred houses, a grammar school, four inns, shops and a brewery, it was the centre of the countryside round about. Nevertheless it had to go. Damer provided a new church and a handsome vicarage in a dry valley to the south-east; he transferred the almshouses built by the Tregonwells, complete with its seventeenth-century façade, and built forty almost identical cottages to flank the long street of his new village. Not surprisingly, the townspeople did not want to move, so over the space of twenty years Damer systematically demolished their houses as each lease expired. Eventually the cottages of the new Milton Abbas were filled with up to four families apiece: it is a tribute to time's healing forgetfulness that such abject misery has been transformed into today's picturesque tranquillity.

In the park that was laid out for Damer by Capability Brown, only one cottage of the old town survives, but the hollows of Broad Street and Fishway Street are well marked, having alongside them the low hummocks that are the sites of vanished houses and gardens.

Other landowners were more constructive: John, Second Duke of Montagu, planned a major new port on the banks of the Beaulieu River. Clearance of the site and the construction of the first roads in Montagu Town began in 1724, but the disastrous failure of one of the Duke's other projects – new sugar plantations on St Lucia – meant that the whole urban enterprise had to be abandoned. Nevertheless, by the time

Top left: A cottage of 'cruck' construction at Lacock. The curved beams could support the ridge of the roof without taking up too much room internally.
Top right: The late eighteenth-century village of Milton Abbas, built to replace the market town destroyed to make way for a landscaped park, neatly fills a dry valley.
Above: Some of the identical cottages built to house the displaced citizens of Milton Abbas town. Each cottage contained two separate dwellings, both entered through the single front door.
Left: John, Second Duke of Montagu, who inherited Beaulieu in 1709. The costly collapse of his scheme to establish lucrative sugar plantations in the West Indies meant that his plans for a major port – Montagu Town – at Buckler's Hard also failed.

of the Duke's death in 1749, there were houses down the broad street to the quayside of what had already begun to be an important ship-building village: Buckler's Hard. Over the next fifty years three dozen naval vessels (with over 1,100 guns) and an even larger number of merchantmen were built there, making good use of the abundant local timber.

Great Houses and Parklands

Less enterprising landowners chose to concentrate much of their time and resources on their great houses and parklands, many of which were centred on the old monastic estates.

The Tudor house at Lacock, with its fine octagonal corner-tower, was 'Gothicized' for the Talbot family in the mid eighteenth century; at Mottisfont the nave of the abbey church had been converted into the core of a large country house in the years after the Dissolution, and in the 1740s was remodelled into its substantial but elegant present form.

Elegance came to Wilton rather earlier, securing for it an important niche in the artistic history of Europe. The Tudor house, built on the site of the abbey granted to the first Earl of Pembroke in 1544, has been almost swamped by its successor. Designed in about 1635 by Isaac de Caus – an assistant to Inigo

Jones – on an even grander scale than was actually achieved, its French interior culminates in the magnificent Double Cube room, lined with portraits by Van Dyke. Not until the early nineteenth century were there any drastic alterations, which were then carried out by James Wyatt. At the same time Wyatt's nephew, Jeffrey Wyatville, was redesigning the interior of the magnificent Elizabethan house at Longleat for the Marquess of Bath. All the rooms around the double courtyard at Longleat look out on the park landscaped by Capability Brown in 1757, and again by Humphrey Repton in 1803; the physical surroundings of a great house were receiving more

emphasis in the eighteenth century.

External sources of finance were being ploughed back into the countryside, using wealth that could employ the best architects and gardeners. The finest of these new eighteenth-century Wessex landscapes is at Stourhead, where the banker Henry Hoare had set himself the task of creating an earthly paradise. The mansion of Stourhead had been built in about 1720 for his father (another Henry) in the new Palladian style, to designs by Colen Campbell. Around it, and in many ways quite separate from it, the younger Henry Hoare sculpted a landscape inspired by the paintings of Claude Lorrain and Nicholas

Poussin. He was following the example of Capability Brown, who had abolished the formal garden to set the houses of his clients directly in their surrounding parks. (Ironically, some of the money must have come from the interest on bank loans taken out by other 'improving' landowners.)

Between 1744 and 1770 Hoare dammed the headwaters of the infant River Stour to create a lake to the south-west of the house, built Classical temples, a grotto dedicated to the Water Nymphs, a 'hermitage' and a graceful five-arched Palladian bridge. Unlike many owners Hoare positively enjoyed the conjunction of the fourteenth-century church of St Peter and the village of Stourton with

Top far left: Wilton House, the home of the Earls of Pembroke, as it was in the early nineteenth century. The seventeenth century house was built by an assistant to Inigo Jones but was much altered by Wyatt.

Top centre left: The Gothic Cottage beside the lake at Stourhead. Probably built in the 1780s the 'Gothic' details were added in 1806. The rhododendrons and azaleas were not in the original planting scheme.

Far left: The Stourhead landscape is focussed on the largest of the temples, the Pantheon, built in 1754. Originally dedicated to Hercules, it was designed to house Rysbrack's statue of the god.

Top left: The Temple of Flora at Stourhead. This Classical temple was the earliest building in Hoare's new Italian landscape; designed by Henry Flitcroft, it was completed in 1746.

Above and top right: Two views of the Stourhead landscape about 1770: the upper shows the Palladian bridge, and both are peopled with guests or visitors walking the lakeside circuit.

the Italian world he had recreated. He even brought in and re-erected the medieval High Cross from Bristol to be a feature in his chosen vistas. Trees and shrubs were carefully selected for their shapes and tones, although these have been added to and replaced by later generations. High on the escarpment, overlooking the lowlands of Somerset, Hoare built the triangular Alfred's Tower, 160 ft (49m) high, commemorating not only that king of Wessex but also the peace with France and the accession of George III. Despite – or perhaps

because of – all these varied influences, Stourhead possesses a magical calm: a quiet, mature and confident celebration of Nature and of English civilization in the eighteenth century.

The Eccentric and the Serious

More eccentric manifestations of this interest in landscape are dotted around the hills of Wessex. The giant cut into the turf above Cerne Abbas may date to Roman times, but the

vogue for white horses elsewhere on the Wessex chalk may not be much older than the mid eighteenth century. In 1778 Lord Abingdon's steward remodelled an existing white horse at Westbury, below Bratton Castle. His creation is sleepy-eyed and wooden enough for Trojans, but the idea caught on: within sixty years, at least five other horses were cut on suitable slopes on the Marlborough Downs and around the Vale of Pewsey. More modest in scale, but equally complex to design and construct, were the many mazes that

The Westbury White Horse, re-cut in 1778 immediately below the ramparts of the Iron Age hill fort of Bratton Castle. The steep, ungrazed slopes of the

were carved from the turf throughout Wessex. Some were cut out at least as early as the seventeenth century but for the most part their origins are obscure. Only two now remain: on St Catherine's Hill in Winchester, and on the downland close to the Wiltshire border at Breamore.

Along the skyline of southern Wessex strange towers sprouted between the mid eighteenth and the early nineteenth centuries, in the same genre as Alfred's Tower at Stourhead. Clavel Tower, at Kimmeridge in Purbeck, and

Luttrell's at Calshot are on the very edge of the sea, while inland there are the 'observatories' at Horton and Charborough Park near Wimborne. The latter was the setting and inspiration of Hardy's tale, *Two on a Tower*. Designed to be looked at as well as looked from, their qualities as eyecatchers are also expressed by the simple architecture of Creech Grange Arch, a folly built about 1740 on the crest of the Purbeck ridge. More enigmatic is the early seventeenth-century 'Pepperbox' with its fine views north-westwards to Salisbury;

its original function is unknown. Perhaps we should not inquire too deeply: the utterly non-utilitarian column in Savernake Forest was set up in 1789 to celebrate George III's return to sanity – somewhat prematurely as it turned out.

There was, however, more serious building work to be done. The old market town of Blandford Forum had been partly destroyed by fire in 1713, but in 1731 almost all the buildings were consumed in an immense conflagration which had started in the house of a tallow

halk escarpment contrast with the well-ordered, rectangular fields so typical of the Parliamentary enclosures.

Left: By the late eighteenth century avenues had replaced the Roman walls of Dorchester but the town had not yet expanded. The oval open space is the site of the castle, where the prison was built in the 1790s.

Below: The Church of St Peter and St Paul at Blandford Forum, bursting with civic pride and renewed self-confidence. Beside it is the monument recalling the rebuilding of the town after the great fire of 1731.

Right: Parham's Mill at Gillingham, Dorset, which Constable visited in 1823. After it was burnt down in 1825, a friend told Constable that 'a huge misshapen, new, bright, brick, modern, improved, patent monster is starting up in its stead'.

chandler. For Blandford this was a blessing in disguise, for among its most prominent citizens were two master-masons, the brothers John and William Bastard. Over the next thirty-five years they rebuilt Blandford as the exquisite Georgian town we see today; the old street-lines were retained but otherwise it was entirely redesigned as a coherent whole. There was even some social planning, with specific house-types and areas allotted to the wealthier professional people and merchants, to the shopkeepers and the middle-classes, and to the artisans. The new buildings have a pleasant uniformity of style that was varied by the clever use of different-coloured brick: only

the elegantly arcaded Town Hall and the fine new parish church were distinguished and dignified by being faced in stone.

The church was the centrepiece in the Blandford that, in the words of the monument in the market-place, had been raised 'like the Phoenix from its Ashes, to its present beautiful and flourishing state'. The reverence and gratitude of mortals elsewhere in Wessex were also expressed in church-building. Among many, only a few examples can be mentioned. Farley, to the east of Salisbury, is a simple and graceful red-brick box, a slice of late seventeenth-century London built in the country to serve the contemporary

almshouses opposite. Urban in design, but also in scale, is the monumental St George's at Reforne on Portland; started in 1754, it has been deserted by its congregation in favour of a more convenient site. A quite different effect was achieved in 1717 when the little seventeenth-century church at Hale was rebuilt. More confident and sophisticated than Portland, it sits hidden in the trees above the Avon Valley to the north of Fordingbridge; well away from the delightful village green, it was convenient for the adjacent mansion of Hale Park.

Greater religious tolerance enabled the nonconformists to build permanent chapels also. The tradition

close proximity of the sheep on the downs and from the presence of water to power its mills. In the late seventeenth century the town entered its heyday, producing heavy felted cloths that achieved an international reputation. With good-quality stone in the hillsides all around, the clothiers were able to build themselves very fine homes, like Westbury House and those in Woolley Street and Silver Street: appropriate names. The grandest of all is Belcombe Court, really a small country house, more akin to the beauty of Bath, in gracefully landscaped grounds on the western edge of the town. However, within two generations of a Palladian wing being added to this mansion in 1734, the life-blood of the town was threatened. By about 1800 it had over thirty mills, but the heavy cloths that they turned out were being rapidly overtaken by the lighter worsteds of Yorkshire.

The textile industry in Salisbury had already dwindled, employing about a quarter of the workforce by 1750. It revived briefly between 1780 and 1810 when, partly due to its willingness to adopt the 'spinning jenny', the manufacture of flannel was extremely successful. However, even in this it could not long compete with the industrialized North which had the coal to fuel the new steam engines. Trowbridge, on the other hand, did have access to the coalfield of Somerset; thus the town could continue its eighteenth-century prosperity, still so evident in the graceful buildings along Fore Street and the Parade. Any disputes that arose between the weavers were settled at the house known as The Courts, at Holt nearby.

For Salisbury, however, the ancient trades carried on the backs of its sheep were dead by the time the young Princess Victoria ascended to the throne. As it eddied quietly into a backwater of the modern world, the future for the region around the little cathedral city lay in the hands of the farmer, the soldier and the tourist.

that the little meeting-house at Horningsham is the one provided for the Scottish Presbyterians engaged to build Longleat – which would make it the earliest surviving chapel in the country – is without foundation; under its thatched roof this charming cottage-like building actually dates to about 1700. The elegant Congregational churches at Lyme Regis (1750) and at Poole (1777), and the former Presbyterian Church (1698) at Bradford-on-Avon bring us back to the towns again, where the denominational and social divides were often acute.

The Woollen Industry

In some ways Wessex was fortunate to experience its industrial revolution earlier than elsewhere; the scars were not so deep and many have healed and been forgotten. Wool was still the basic commodity. While at Dorchester the industry was declining, half the workforce of Salisbury was still engaged in textiles in the mid seventeenth century; the fragile but continuing prosperity of the city is reflected by such buildings as Mompesson House. The perfect Queen Anne home, its stone façade gently dominates the Chorister's Green in the Close at Salisbury, the centrepiece of a pleasing jumble of architectural styles.

Like Salisbury, Bradford-on-Avon had also benefited from the

MODERN TIMES

Down beside the seaside a new industry was stirring along the fringes of Wessex. In the mid eighteenth century persons of quality discovered that Britain was surrounded by sea water and by beaches, and that moreover these could be extremely pleasant things.

THE KING REWARDING THE INDUSTRIOUS HAYMAKER NEAR WEYMOUTH.

By 1750 bathing machines had been installed on the sands at Melcombe Regis (now the northern portion of Weymouth). Thirty years later the Duke of Gloucester chose to spend the winter there, building himself Gloucester Lodge (now an hotel) directly on the Esplanade and establishing the town as a fashionable resort. In 1789 George III visited Melcombe, liked what he saw and came regularly for over twenty years. Royal patronage and the presence of the Court created a new prosperity and the town expanded rapidly; the boom lasted until about 1850 and is marked by the elegant Georgian terraces, with their balconies or shallow bow windows, all along the sea front.

The bathers on Weymouth sands could not long forget the most ominous threat of the day: the possibility of a Napoleonic invasion. Coastal defences were strengthened and local defence volunteers were organized to supplement the militia and the army: elaborate contingency plans were drawn up and the numerous false alarms caused much panic. One relic of this time is the cottage known as Bramshaw Telegraph, at the northern tip of the New Forest near Redlynch, which was one of a chain of semaphore stations linking the south coast with London. More obvious reminders include the early eighteenth-century mansion at Standlynch near Salisbury, which was renamed Trafalgar and given by the nation to Nelson's heirs. Close to the Dorset coast is the monument to Sir Thomas Hardy, flag-captain of HMS *Victory*, who was born at Portesham nearby. At Portland, within sight of the monument, are the breakwaters of the new deep-water anchorage for the Navy's increasingly large ships; these took twenty-five years to complete and were not finished until 1872.

The end of the Napoleonic Wars brought in a sudden agricultural slump in which many farmers went bankrupt. Starvation wages and long hours, especially on the big estates,

eventually triggered off the wave of rick-burning and machinery-breaking known as the 'Captain Swing' riots of 1830. However, the concessions won were soon eroded and the desperation in Dorset was expressed by the formation of the Friendly Society of Agricultural Labourers, at Tolpuddle in 1834. Again the magistrates had the upper hand: to our eyes it may seem ironic that the 'martyrs' of this still-born and illegitimate trade union were transported by the newly reformed House of Commons that no longer contained such democratic absurdities as a Member for Old Sarum.

By the 1840s the land was prospering again; in the accelerating drift away from sheep much of the old downland was broken up and woollen mills had to be converted to other uses. At Wilton production was switched to carpets in 1830 and at Bradford-on-Avon Stephen Moulton had the courage to capitalize on the new invention of vulcanized rubber. Although the fine Abbey Mill of 1875 marks a last brave attempt to revitalize the town's traditional industry it was Avon Rubber that held the key to prosperity. Another future industry had germinated at Lacock Abbey, where in 1835 Fox Talbot had successfully developed the first photographic negative.

Top: King George III on his charger, cut out of the turf of the chalk downland at Osmington, near Weymouth, in 1808. Nearly 330 ft (100 m) high, it celebrates the king's patronage of the booming seaside resort.
Above centre: The monument on Black Down, near Dorchester, to Sir Thomas Hardy, flag-captain of the *Victory* at Trafalgar. It has been described as a 'factory chimney with a crinoline', but the views from it are magnificent.
Centre: Heywood House, a small mid-Victorian country seat near Westbury: solid, confident and neo-Jacobean.
Above left: Abbey Mill, Bradford-on-Avon, the last of the great woollen mills in the town. It has now been converted into offices and a restaurant.
Left: A very early view of Lacock Abbey by the pioneer photographer, Fox Talbot. It was here that in 1835 he developed the first photographic negative.

Canals and Railways

Wiltshire cheese and bacon had been
sent to London in the eighteenth
century but it was the coming of the
canals and of the railways that
provided a stimulus to the dairy
industry and allowed cattle to take
the place of sheep. Wessex was
infected with 'canal fever' at the end
of the eighteenth century but the
impact of the new waterways was not
as dramatic as elsewhere; indeed
some of the early attempts to open up
the agricultural hinterland of
Christchurch and Southampton were
disastrous failures. The Avon was
briefly made navigable as far as
Salisbury in the late seventeenth
century, and in the 1790s a canal was
begun to link the city with the
Andover Canal and thus with
Southampton. Both schemes failed,
one because of too much water, the
other because of too little money.

 The most successful
waterway was cut across northern
Wessex, linking Newbury and Bath
via the Vale of Pewsey. Completed in
1810, the major obstacle to the Kennet
and Avon Canal was the steep fall of
nearly 240 ft (73 m) between
Semington and Devizes, for which 29
locks were required: the 'staircase' of
17 locks down Caen Hill on the west
side of the town is still impressive.
Further east, the pumping station at
Crofton near Great Bedwyn retains
one of its original Boulton and Watt
steam beam-engines, installed in
1812. Wharves at Burbage, Pewsey,
and Honey Street near Alton Barnes,
still active with narrow-boat traffic,
have some of the atmosphere of inland
ports but the heyday of the canals was
brief and they were soon bought out
by the railways.

 Development in the railway
age was rapid. Brunel's Great Western
Railway linked London with Bath in
1844; by 1860 Salisbury was a major
junction with lines to Southampton,
London, Exeter and Bath. The line
through Somerset and Dorset to
Weymouth was complete by 1857,

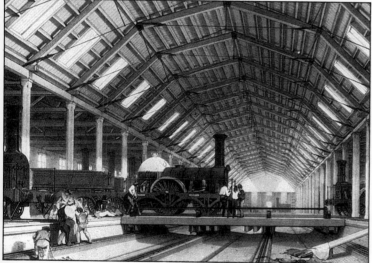

scale, occurred around the works at Eastleigh, which took its name from a nearby farm.

All this pales in comparison with the phenomenal growth of Bournemouth. In 1811, Lewis Tregonwell, a member of the Dorset family who had bought Milton Abbas at the Dissolution and built the fine Jacobean manor at Anderson near Bere Regis, chose a site for a summer home in the heathlands by the sea. The only other building nearby was an inn; but in 1837 Sir George Tapps-Gervis realized that this sheltered bay would be perfect for a seaside resort. The beginnings were modest: in 1851 the population was under 700, but the arrival of the railway in 1870 attracted more visitors to enjoy the scenery and the climate, so that by 1901 there were 59,000 people in the town. The conurbation has now swallowed the ancient boroughs of Christchurch and Poole; extending for about 14 miles (22 km) along the coast, it has a population of about 300,000.

The picture was not the same elsewhere; in the countryside the young people were leaving for the more prosperous towns. Beaminster's population fell by a third between 1871 and 1901, reflecting the overall decline in the wealth of the area. A measure of this is the slump in the numbers of sheep which in Dorset fell by about forty per cent in the second half of the nineteenth century. By the end of the Second World War they amounted to only a tenth of what they had been a century before.

Above left: The lush meadows of Blackmoor Vale are prime dairy country.
Left: Bradford-on-Avon in the early nineteenth century: a townscape of mills and rich houses. The Kennet and Avon Canal runs in the foreground, with the River Avon beyond. The great monastic barn at Barton Farm occupies the bottom right and the Hall, home of the Moultons, rises above the small wood at centre right.
Top: The new railway town of Swindon in about 1850, showing the locomotive works at the junction with the Cheltenham line and, on the right, the 'village' of terraced cottages built by the Great Western Railway with stone dug out for the great tunnel at Box between Chippenham and Bath. The station lies in the middle distance.
Above: The Engine House, at Swindon in 1845, illustrating the enormous investment required for the complex business of building and maintaining locomotives.

providing on the outskirts of Dorchester two early examples of environmental conservation enforced by pressure groups: a tunnel under the hill fort of Poundbury and a tight curve to avoid Maumbury Rings. The most dramatic effect of course was at Swindon, where the site chosen for the Great Western's engineering workshops was about a mile away from the old village with its population of about 2,000. The original sheds have been modernized, but the stone terrace cottages of the village built by the company for its workforce in the 1840s and 1850s have been sympathetically restored. A similar development, on a slightly smaller

Literary Landscapes

In spite of all this, the well-to-do Victorians were still able to indulge their passion for the building and restoration of churches. T. H. Wyatt, the consultant architect of the Salisbury Diocesan Church Building Association, built, rebuilt, or restored no less than sixty churches, in various styles of Gothic between the 1830s and the 1860s. A younger architect in the diocese, Thomas Hardy, was also

restoring churches, including St Peter's, Dorchester, and West Knighton not far away. His architecture is worthy, but no match for his poetry and prose.

Few writers can be so closely identified with an area as Hardy is with Wessex, for he placed his heroes and heroines in a thinly-disguised Dorset landscape that is familiar and well-loved. Hardy was born at Higher Bockhampton (Tranter Dewy's cottage in *Under the Greenwood Tree*), close to Stinsford (Mellstock) where his heart is buried. His later life was spent at Dorchester (Casterbridge) nearby, where he made the mayor, Michael Trenchard, play out his fated tale; not far away Puddletown is still synonymous with Bathsheba Everdene's Weatherbury, and Tess and Angel Clare spent their wedding night at Woolbridge Manor. Further north, W. H. Hudson chronicled the life of a shepherd, Caleb Balcombe, on the downs of south Wiltshire and Cranborne Chase, and Richard Jefferies drew out the essence of the Marlborough Downs.

The Soldier, the Farmer and the Tourist

The rural world of those writers was shattered by the impact of the twentieth century. Defence again became a priority for Wessex and in 1897 the heart of Salisbury Plain was requisitioned for military training. Despite assurances, Imber became (and remains) a ghost village, only to be followed by Tyneham in western Purbeck. At Fovant regimental badges were carved into the turf and New Zealanders cut a kiwi out of the face of the down above the barracks at Bulford. Airfields were built on the heathland plateaux of the New Forest, and Buckler's Hard was again in use for naval vessels. The beaches at Studland saw the rehearsals for the Normandy landings, and the Saxon defences at Wareham were recut

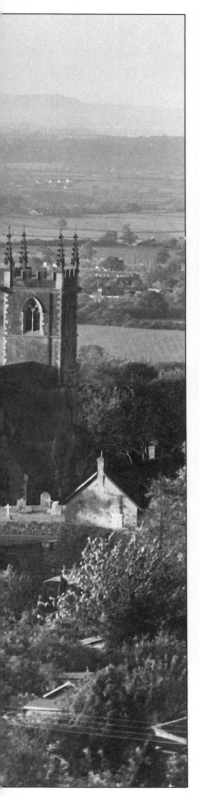

Left: The western outskirts of Shaftesbury, looking down from Castle Hill. The houses date from the sixteenth to the nineteenth centuries and St James's Church was rebuilt in 1866 by T. H. Wyatt, incorporating parts of its medieval predecessor.

Top: Thomas Hardy in middle age, at the height of his powers as a novelist. For most of his life he lived in or close to Dorchester, surrounded by the Wessex countryside from which his characters were drawn.

Above: The eighteenth-century cottage at Higher Bockhampton where Thomas Hardy was born in 1840. Here he wrote *Far From the Madding Crowd* and *Under the Greenwood Tree* – in which this cottage is the home of Tranter Dewy.

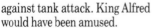

against tank attack. King Alfred would have been amused.

In our late twentieth-century world Wessex has seen many changes and contradictions. The downland has been put to the plough as never before, while in the valleys the fish-farms and watercress beds flourish. Cattle and creameries have replaced sheep, and mushrooms are grown commercially in the disused quarries of Bradford-on-Avon. Each year the motorways and arterial roads pull the cities closer and a thousand tons of litter is removed from the New Forest. Salisbury diocese has more redundant churches than any other, but increased mobility and earlier retirement have saved thousands of cottages from dereliction. Oil and gas have been tapped from the southern edge of Poole Harbour, although Salisbury was still generating its electricity from the water flowing under the Town Mill when the atomic power station on Winfrith Heath was opened. Insurance and computing have become local industries, and greater leisure and affluence have meant that the 8,000 moorings for small boats between Lyme Bay and Southampton Water are no longer enough.

In the forbidden lands around Lulworth Cove the rare wild cabbage has sprung up in the shell-holes, and on Bovington Heath the deep trenches gouged out by the tanks have been colonized by the Dartford Warbler.

Above left: A stretch of the M4 between Wroughton and Chiseldon, near Swindon, looking east towards the edge of the downland with Burderop Wood in the foreground.
Above: The medieval church at Imber on Salisbury Plain in 1807. The inhabitants of this battle-torn ghost village-a 'Wessex Pompeii'-had six weeks' notice to leave in 1943, surrendering their homes to an army training area.
Right: Clouds Hill, the austere little cottage near Bovington Camp in Dorset where T.E. Lawrence (of Arabia) worked on *The Seven Pillars of Wisdom.* In 1935 he was living in retirement there when he was killed in a motorcycle accident nearby.

ACKNOWLEDGMENTS

The publishers are grateful to Richard Muir who took most of the photographs. Other illustrations were kindly provided by:

Aerofilms Ltd 34; 35; 38 bottom; 39 bottom.
Cambridge University Collection of Air Photographs 15 centre; 17; 19 centre; 37; 38 top; 42 top; 43 bottom; 45; 59 bottom; 64; 66; 70 top; 72; 77 top right; 91 top.
Great Western Railway Museum, Swindon 87 both.
Kennet-Avon Canal Trust 86 bottom.
Mansell Collection 77 bottom; 84; 89 top.
National Trust 15 top; 69; 70 bottom; 74; 75; 78 top right and bottom; 79 all; 85 bottom; 89 bottom; 91 bottom.
Salisbury and South Wiltshire Museum 41 bottom.
Wiltshire Archaeological and Natural History Society 11, William Stukeley *Itinerarium Curiosum;* 15 bottom, Stukeley; 19 left, Sir Richard Colt-Hoare *Ancient Wiltshire;* 22 bottom, Stukeley; 23 bottom, Colt-Hoare; 28, Colt-Hoare; 30 both; 36, Colt-Hoare; 39 top, Stukeley; 39 middle, Colt-Hoare; 41 top, Colt-Hoare; 44, William Stukeley *North Wiltshire;* 68 bottom, Stukeley; 78 top left by J. C. Buckler; 82 left, J Hutchins *History of Dorset;* 90 by J. C. Buckler.
Woodmansterne Ltd 46; 47; 67; 83.
Illustration on 55 from *The Ancient Earthworks of the New Forest* by Heywood Sumner. Map on 14 by Stephen Gyapay.

FURTHER READING

Affairs of state have rarely intruded into this short history of a changing rural landscape and of some of its people. The classic account of this approach to the past is W.G. Hoskins's **The Making of the English Landscape**: continuously reprinted since its first appearance in 1955, it never fails to excite the imagination and to fire enthusiasm. Following the same path is Christopher Taylor's **Village and Farmstead** (1983), subtitled 'A History of Rural Settlement in England'; the author knows Wessex well and takes many of his examples from the area.

Wessex also looms large in the archaeology and early history of these islands: detailed summaries of recent research can be found in the **Introduction to British Prehistory** edited by J.V.S. Megaw and D.D.A Simpson (1979) and in **Roman Britain** by Peter Salway (1981). Some of the same ground is covered in a more popular way by R. Muir and H. Welfare in the **National Trust Guide to Prehistoric and Roman Britain** (1983). Books on individual prehistoric subjects in Wessex include: **Stonehenge** by R.J.C. Atkinson (1979); **Stonehenge Complete** by Christopher Chippendale (1983); **Prehistoric Avebury** by Aubrey Burl (1979), and Barry Cunliffe's **Hengistbury Head** (1978) and **Danebury: the anatomy of an Iron Age hillfort** (1983). David Wilson has written the most accessible account of **The Anglo-Saxons** (3rd ed., 1981), and Wessex has been particularly well-served by David Hinton's **Alfred's Kingdom: Wessex and the South 800–1500** (1977).

The Victoria County Histories have been published for **Hampshire** (1900–12) but **Dorset** is still unfinished (3 volumes, the latest in 1968), as is Wiltshire (11 volumes up to 1980). Much of the groundwork was done by the major nineteenth-century county histories: **The History of Dorset** by J. Hutchins (1864) and Sir Richard Colt Hoare's huge **History of Modern Wiltshire** (1822–43) and his **Ancient Wiltshire** (1810, 1821).

More detailed treatment of the landscape is provided by Christopher Taylor's **Dorset** (1970) in the **Making of the English Landscape** series, and also by J.P. Williams-Freeman in **An Introduction to Field Archaeology as illustrated by Hampshire** (1915) – although this is now very out of date in many respects. All the ancient buildings and earthworks of Dorset have been exhaustively recorded by the Royal Commission on Historical Monuments (England) in its **Inventory of the Historical Monuments of Dorset,** published in several volumes between 1952 and 1975. Other Wessex studies from the same source include **Stonehenge and its Environs** (1979) and **Salisbury City** (1980). Penguin's famous **Buildings of England** series provides accurate thumbnail architectural descriptions: **Dorset** by J. Newman and N. Pevsner (1972), **Hampshire** by N. Pevsner and D. Lloyd (1967), and **Wiltshire** by N. Pevsner and B. Cherry (1975).

Some counter-balance to all this quiet but civilized descriptive prose is provided by accounts of the people themselves in J.H. Bettey's **Dorset** (1974) and John Chandler's excellent **Endless Street: a history of Salisbury and its people** (1983).

Our knowledge of the history and archaeology of Wessex is being constantly extended and revised. The county societies (membership of which is inexpensive and warmly recommended) provide a vital role by publishing most of this new information: the Dorset Natural History and Archaeological Society in Dorchester, the Hampshire Field Club in Winchester, and the Wiltshire Archaeological and Natural History Society in Devizes.

Maps Finally, no explorer should go without the Ordnance Survey's Landranger (1:50,000) or Pathfinder (1:25,000) maps, or the two special Outdoor Leisure maps of **Purbeck** and of **The New Forest.**

INDEX

Page numbers in italics refer to illustrations.